How
Fiction
Works

How Fiction Works

The last word on writing fiction—
from basics to the fine points.

OAKLEY HALL

STORY PRESS
CINCINNATI, OHIO
www.writersdigest.com

Visit our Web site at www.writersdigest.com for information on more resources for writers.

To receive a free weekly e-mail newsletter delivering tips and updates about writing and about Writer's Digest products, send an e-mail with the message "Subscribe Newsletter" to newsletter-request@writersdigest.com, or register directly at our Web site at www.writersdigest.com.

05   04   03   02   01   5   4   3   2   1

Library of Congress Cataloging-in-Publication Data

Hall, Oakley M.
    How fiction works / by Oakley Hall.
        p.   cm.
    Includes index.
    ISBN 1-88491-049-1 (alk. paper)
        1. Fiction—Authorship. I. Title.

PN3355 .H29   2000
808.3—dc21   00-061879
                                                                  CIP

Edited by Jack Heffron and Michelle Howry
Interior designed by Sandy Kent
Production coordinated by Emily Gross

For Hunter Dallas Jones

🐚 About the Author 🐚

O akley Hall was born in San Diego, attended the University of California at Berkeley (B.A.) and the University of Iowa (M.F.A.). He served in the Marines in World War II. He and his wife, the photographer Barbara Hall, have four children and seven grandchildren. They live half the year in San Francisco and half in Squaw Valley in the Sierra. He has published twenty-one novels, two of which, *Warlock* and *The Downhill Racers*, were made into major motion pictures. *Separations* was a winner of a Southwest Book Award. He is a recipient of the Spur Award of the Western Writers of America. He wrote the libretto for the opera *Angle of Repose* (adapted from the Wallace Stegner novel), which was San Francisco Opera's Bicentenniel Offering, and a writing text, *The Art and Craft of Novel Writing*. He was for twenty-two years director of the programs in writing at the University of California at Irvine, and for thirty years general director of a summer writers conference, the Squaw Valley Community of Writers. He has been inducted into the Cowboy Hall of Fame (1989) and is the recipient of a PEN-West Award of Honor (1998).

❧ Books by Oakley Hall ❧

Novels

So Many Doors, 1950
Corpus of Joe Bailey, 1953
Mardios Beach, 1955
Warlock, 1958
The Downhill Racers, 1962
The Pleasure Garden, 1966
Report From Beau Harbor, 1972
The Adelita, 1975
The Bad Lands, 1978
Lullaby, 1982
The Children of the Sun, 1983
The Coming of the Kid, 1985
Apaches, 1986
Separations, 1997

Mystery Novels

Murder City (as O.M. Hall), 1949
Too Dead To Run (as Jason Manor), 1953
The Red Jaguar (as Jason Manor), 1954
The Pawns of Fear (as Jason Manor), 1955
The Tramplers (as Jason Manor), 1956
A Game for Eagles (as Oakley Hall), 1970
Ambrose Bierce and the Queen of Spades (as Oakley Hall), 1998
Ambrose Bierce and the Death of Kings (in press), 2001

Other

Libretto for the opera *Angle of Repose*
   (from the novel by Wallace Stegner), 1976
The Art and Craft of Novel Writing, 1989

❧ Table *of* Contents ❧

❧ Introduction ❧

When asked a few years ago, as a novelist and teacher of writing, for a list of writing tips to accompany a publicity piece in a San Francisco newspaper, I produced the following list:

1. Write every day.
2. Observe and listen.
3. Employ all the senses.
4. Use strong verbs.
5. Detail!
6. A specific always beats an abstraction.
7. Describe in motion.
8. Anglo-Saxon words are usually more effective than romance based.
9. Fiction is dramatization; dramatization is point of view, sense impressions, detail, action and dialogue.
10. In dialogue, keep speeches short.
11. Look for likenesses, parallels, contrasts, antitheses and reversals.
12. Beware the use of the habitual case (*would*), the passive voice and the word *there*.
13. Plotting is compulsion versus obstacles.
14. In the second draft, start deleting adverbs.
15. Borrow widely, steal wisely.

I have been a writer all of my adult life. My first novel was published in 1949, my latest in 1998—twenty-one in all: mainstream, historicals, westerns and mysteries. Two of them have been made into major motion pictures. I've also published short stories, novelettes, an opera libretto, some pieces of a memoir, a little travel and a book on novel writing.

I taught fiction writing for twenty-two years at the University of California at Irvine, where I was Director of the Programs in Writing, and have been Director of the Squaw Valley Community of Writers, a summer writers conference, for thirty years. Do I know it all? Not a bit. Still learning.

Since my young years as a student at Columbia and the University of Iowa, I have collected pieces of writing, words, sentences, paragraphs and pages of action, description, characterization, symbol, setting and plot that seemed to work and where I could understand how and why they worked. It is through these examples that I hope, in this book, to show you what good writing is and how it can be accomplished. Many a new writer, in his own reading career, will recognize terrific stuff when he casts his eye on it. This book is aimed at assisting him in making the switch from reading it to writing it.

❧ PART I ❧

The Dramatic Method

My task which I am trying to achieve is, by the power of the written word, to make you hear, to make you feel—it is before all to make you see. That—and no more, and it is everything.

—JOSEPH CONRAD, *PREFACES*

❧ CHAPTER 1 ❧

Specification

If those who have studied the art of writing are in accord on one point it is on this: the surest way to arouse and hold the reader is to be specific, definite, and concrete.

—*THE ELEMENTS OF STYLE*

Concrete vs. abstract
Specific vs. general
Particular vs. ill-defined
Individual vs. type
Peculiar vs. generic
Precise vs. ambiguous
Detailed vs. summarized
Definite vs. indefinite
Distinct vs. indistinct

These oppositions may not all be perfect, but I hope the distinctions are clear. Fiction lives on the specific, the particular. It dies on the abstract and the general, such as: "Local man appointed to post."

Aristotle wrote that Homer "first taught the rest of us the art of framing lies the right way." In this passage from *The Odyssey* (Robert Fagles's translation), the goddess Athena has come to Ithaca to look in on the situation Telemachus is going to have to deal with. Notice the specific detail in which Homer frames his lies:

> There she found the swaggering suitors, just then
> amusing themselves with rolling dice before the doors,

lounging on hides of oxen they had killed themselves.
While heralds and brisk attendants bustled round them,
some at the mixing-bowls, mulling wine and water,
others wiping the tables down with sopping sponges,
setting them out in place, still other servants
jointed and carved the great sides of meat.

Speaking of his very popular historical novel *Cold Mountain*, the author Charles Frazier said of it: "One thing people like—and it's something I worked real hard on—is the physical texture of another time and place." In the above passage from *The Odyssey*, a historical novel, Homer is working hard to give us the physical texture of that time and place.

Here is Ellen Gilchrist, trotting out specifics in the beginning of her short story "The Last Diet":

On the twenty-fourth day of August, nineteen hundred and eighty-five, JeanAnne Lori Mayfield, third child and only daughter of Mr. and Mrs. Johnny Wayne Mayfield of Fayetteville, Arkansas, ended her last and final diet by running her navy blue Toyota sedan into a doughnut shop. She could have swerved the other way and hit the emergency entrance of the Washington County General Hospital, but, no, she plowed into the front window of Daytime Doughnuts, Number Three, killing a waitress, an overweight professor of English at the university, and herself.

Barbara Kingsolver specifies at the beginning of her short story "Islands on the Moon":

Annemarie's mother, Magda, is one of a kind. She wears sandals and one-hundred-percent cotton dresses and walks like she's crossing plowed ground. She makes necklaces from the lacquered vertebrae of non-endangered species. Her hair is wavy and threaded with gray. She's forty-four.

Kingsolver makes the abstract statement that Magda is one of a kind, then sets out to prove it with specific information.

Notice the specific opening paragraph of Thackeray's *Vanity Fair*:

> While the present century was in its teens, and on one sunshiny morning in June, there drove up to the great iron gate of Miss Pinkerton's academy for young ladies, on Chiswick Mall, a large family coach, with two fat horses in blazing harness, driven by a fat coachman in a three-cornered hat and wig, at the rate of four miles an hour.

Toni Morrison is specific in this description from her novel *Paradise*. Mavis has picked up a hitchhiker. It is during the Vietnam War:

> The girl said her name—Sandra but call me Dusty—and talked for thirty-two miles. Not interested in anything about Mavis. Dusty ate two Mallomars and chattered, mostly about the owners of the six dog tags that hung from her neck. Boys in her high school class or whom she had known in junior high. She'd got two when they dated; the rest she begged from their families—souvenirs. All dead or missing.

The reader is kept continuingly aware of Dusty's presence by "the clink of dog tags."

The specific details here, the thirty-two miles, two Mallomars, six dog tags—two from dates—are very effective. The realization that Dusty has begged dog tags from the parents of boys dead or MIA in Vietnam adds to the mood of slow horror that Morrison is building in this chapter.

This passage is from the short story "The Haunted Beach" by Alice Adams:

> That night she and Ben walk into town for dinner . . . , and they find the town very much as it was: dingy, rutted, poorly lit streets leading toward the center, along which wary old men loiter, sometimes stopping to rest on the stoop of a darkened house, to smoke a cigarette, to stare at the night. Then stores, small and shabby at first, little groceries, ill-equipped drugstores with timid souvenirs, faded postcards, cheap cosmetics. And then more light, larger and gaudier stores. More people. The same old mix

of tourists, always identifiable as non-Mexican. And Mexicans, mostly poor, some very poor, beggars, pitiful dark thin women, holding babies.

Alice Adams was an accomplished and graceful writer but (to my mind) has not given this description enough attention. There is not one specific or vivid detail here; all is general, abstract, adjectival: *"ill-equipped* drug-stores," *"timid* souvenirs," *"faded* postcards," *"cheap* cosmetics." None of these have any visual impact except perhaps for the faded postcards, which, however, would not be visible in the darkness. People who appear in the scene are all generalized; no particular person is shown. One recalls Chekhov's advice to a young writer who has described a pocketful of change: "Just show me one penny hopping and chinking."

The next passage is from Jon Krakauer's *Into Thin Air*, a history of the 1996 Mount Everest climbing disasters. It is a list of the author's fellow climbers. It should be noted that this is nonfiction and the author is not subject to fictional demands. This list is specific in a very different way than would be required in a work of fiction:

> . . . there was Helen Wilson, a thirty-nine-year-old mother of four, who was returning for her third season as Base Camp Manager. Caroline Mackenzie—an accomplished climber and physician in her late twenties—was the expedition doctor and, like Helen, would be going no higher than Base Camp. Lou Kasischke, the gentlemanly lawyer I'd met at the airport, had climbed six of the Seven Summits—as had Yasuko Namba, forty-seven, a taciturn personnel director who worked at the Tokyo branch of Federal Express. Beck Weathers, forty-nine, was a garrulous pathologist from Dallas. Stuart Hutchison, thirty-four, attired in a Ren and Stimpy T-shirt, was a cerebral, somewhat wonkish Canadian cardiologist on leave from a re-search fellowship. John Taske, at fifty-six the oldest member of our group, was an anesthesiologist from Brisbane who'd taken up climbing after retiring from the Australian Army. Frank Fischbeck, fifty-three, a dapper, genteel publisher from

Hong Kong . . . Doug Hansen, forty-six, was an American postal worker. . . .

There would seem to be a generous supply of specifics here, names, ages, professions, nationality. But in fact these are all abstractions. None of these people has been induced to breathe. There is no picture. Joseph Conrad pointed out the writer's responsiblity "to make you see." There is nothing to see here as yet but the Ren and Stimpy T-shirt. We have the climbers' names, ages, origins and careers. None of this is vivid or dramatic in the reader's mind, except, perhaps, for that T-shirted Canadian.

Abstract vs. Specific

1. Some people came into the room.
2. Three women and a tiny jockey in orange silks crowded through the gate.

1. He was a big man with a beard.
2. He filled the doorway, his beard glistening with curls.

1. It was cold in the kitchen.
2. She hunched her shoulders and rubbed her hands together against the chill in the kitchen.

1. The crowd passed in the street.
2. The street brimmed with the jostling of men in cloth caps and women in babushkas.

1. The baby lay in his crib.
2. In the blue crib the pink and gurgling child made knitting motions with his plump fists.

1. The man walked across the floor.
2. The burly security man hastened across the black and white tiles.

Here is a character's description from P.D. James's *Death of an Expert Witness*:

Angela Foley presented a bland, inscrutable gaze. She was an unusual-looking girl with a heart-shaped face and a wide, exceedingly high forehead from which hair, baby fine, the color of ripe grain, was strained back and plaited into a tight coil on top of her head. Her eyes were narrow, slanted, and so deeply set that Dalgliesh found it hard to guess their color. Her mouth was small, pursed, and uncommunicative above the pointed chin. She wore a dress in fine fawn wool, topped with an elaborately patterned short-sleeved tabard, and short laced boots. . . .

P.D. James's descriptions are always filled with vivid and imaginative data. Perhaps there are more here than is necessary, but these details are given from Chief Inspector Dalgliesh's point of view, and Dalgliesh is examining witnesses looking for revelations, clues, *information*.

The above description would have been more effective put into motion, in action. An image in motion is more striking than a static one.

See E.L. Doctorow incorporating this writerly basic in his novel *The Waterworks*. The narrator is giving this description:

A commanding figure, not tall, but military in his bearing . . . slender stature with the stillness of consummate self-confidence . . . wearing the customary frock coat, slightly puffed at the shoulder seams, and the vest with fabric-covered buttons, and the wide loosely tied cravat with stickpin. The overall impression is of neatness, self-containment. Thick black hair cut short. His cheeks and upper lip and chin are clean-shaven, but burnsides frame his jaw and continue under his chin and curl around the throat like a woolen scarf tucked in under the collar. Black, implacable eyes, surprisingly opaque, with a kind of desolation in them—a harsh impersonality, reminding me of Sherman, William Tecumseh Sherman. Good rounded forehead, slightly domed, thin, straight nose, thin-lipped, absemptious mouth. *I'll animate him with an action: He holds a watch on a fob, glances at it, and slips it back into his vest pocket.* (Emphasis added.)

Doctorow has put his character in motion. It may have been more effective to activate him before the abundance of detail, for the reader's eye would have been much more involved than in what is static description. However, the action into which this description is animated is emblematic of the character, and indeed of the theme of the novel, which is mortality.

Both of the above pieces are dense with detail. How much detail is necessary? Fiction depends upon the selection of detail, not the amassing of it, and after the writer's job as an observer is finished, his job as a selector begins. Which of the details applying to his character are the most striking and effective?

The Rule of Three

Henry James's fictional dictum was "Select, contemplate, render": Select the detail, contemplate how best to use it, render it—dramatize it in motion or significance.

One detail, if exquisitely chosen, may serve to bring the breath of life. Or two. Four or more details often means the author has not selected well enough.

Robert Jordan views the bridge he has been ordered to blow up, in Hemingway's *For Whom the Bell Tolls* (numbers are mine):

> It was wide enough for two cars to pass (1) and it spanned, in solid-flung metal grace (2), a deep gorge at the bottom of which, far below, a brook leaped in white water through rocks and boulders down to the main stream of the pass (3).

Herbert Gold introduces his principal female character in his novel *She Took My Arm as if She Loved Me*:

> . . . a careless insulation of extra flesh that would soon melt off, since it was unneeded by a fast-moving athlete; yellowish square teeth which got brightness from their intensity of use in grinning; hugely amused avid—that's *hungry* blue eyes; a look of turbulent health for which youth was only partly to blame.

Priscilla has already been shown in action before this description. There is some abstract description here, but the essential three details are Priscilla's "insulation of extra flesh," "yellowish square teeth" and "hungry blue eyes," details that give this troublesome young woman breath.

In the following passage from Louis B. Jones's *California's Over*, the protagonist has just encountered his long-lost, unknown in fact, twenty-four-year-old son:

> He's tall, taller than I. His hair is cropped short like a mental patient's, which is fashionable now in San Francisco, and his body is fashionably mutilated: a metal grommet is installed in his earlobe and another one in a pinch of skin at his eyebrow. On these grommets he hangs unbent paper clips, fishing lures, flash cards portraying human anatomical features, a rabbit's foot, tampons, used-looking tampons, whatever strikes him as witty that morning. He's an artist.

Again, these three details—his height, his hair and the body-pierced grommets and their cargo—are very vivid. If the boy were just "tall," it would be of not much visual assistance, but "taller than I" gives some specificity. The hair is not just "cropped" but "cropped short like a mental patient's," and the designed-to-shock grommet display is effective and dramatic.

Here's the beginning of Alice Walker's story "Everyday Use":

> I will wait for her in the yard that Maggie and I made so clean and wavy yesterday afternoon. A yard like this is more comfortable than most people know. It is not just a yard. It is like an extended living room. When the hard clay is swept clean as a floor and the fine sand around the edges lined with tiny, irregular grooves, anyone can come and sit and look up into the elm tree and wait for the breezes that never come inside the house.

After several sentences, abstractly reporting the comfort of the yard, Walker gets down to specifics and renders it: the tiny, irregular grooves edging the hard clay floor, the soaring elm tree, the breezes that play in the tree.

Here, Harry Potter's friend-to-be, Hermione, is first presented with three details (although not very well dramatized), in *Harry Potter and the Sorcerer's Stone* by J.K. Rowling:

> She had a bossy sort of voice, lots of bushy hair, and rather large front teeth.

The following description is from Neal Stephenson's *Cryptonomicon*. Goto Dengo is assembling a Filipino work crew to bury the Japanese gold treasure in the Philippines during World War II.

> Goto Dengo has been commanding men long enough, now, that he picks the good ones right away. There is a toothless, pop-eyed character named Rodolfo with iron-grey hair and a big cyst on his cheek, arms that are too long, hands like grappling hooks, and splay-toed feet that remind him of the natives he lived with on New Guinea. His eyes are no particular color— they seem to have been put together from shards of other people's eyes, scintillas of grey, blue, hazel, and black all sintered together. Rodolfo is self-conscious about his lack of teeth and always holds one of his sprawling, prehensile paws over his mouth when he speaks. Whenever Goto Dengo or another authority figure comes nearby, all of the young Filipino men avert their gaze and look significantly at Rodolfo, who steps forward, covers his mouth, and fixes his weird, alarming stare upon the visitor.

Stephenson, in his exuberance, gives the reader more than she really needs in this description of Rodolfo, a very minor character. The detail of covering his mouth to hide bad teeth is an effective one, as are the weird eyes. Most effective is the fact that all the other Filipinos look to him when an authority figure comes by.

In this scene from Richard Ford's *Independence Day*, Frank Bascombe has come to visit his young daughter, who lives with Frank's ex-wife and the ex-wife's new husband:

> Clarissa, in brilliant red shorts over her blue Speedo suit, jumps

up and gives me her hammer hug, and I swing her like a tether-ball before letting her sink weak-kneed into the grass. She has a wonderful smell—dampness and girlish perfume applied hours before, now faded.

Ford has not only put Clarissa into motion, he has given her vivid colors and a smell. "Don't forget the smells!" was John Cheever's advice to his writing students, and this smell is a clincher in making Clarissa *be there*. In fact, there is also another sense employed, that of touch—the girl's hammer hug.

CHAPTER 2

The Senses

All art, therefore, appeals primarily to the senses, and the artistic aim when expressing itself in written words also makes its appeal to the senses.
—JOSEPH CONRAD, *PREFACES*

If there is a profound secret to good writing, it lies in the engagement of the senses.

The poet Jorie Graham describes how a poem develops for her (from an interview in the July 14, 1997, *New Yorker*):

> . . . then there's a little something that comes through. The way the sunlight is striking the snow—it's almost always a sense perception of some kind. Then I just wait. Some other physical things maybe stick to it. Maybe the sun on the snow, and then, the next day, the bright sound of—I don't know, I've never written this poem, so I'm just making this up—but of a crow in an empty winter day snapping a twig. That brightness and that sharpness. And that sort of sticks, because there's a sound element to the image. . . .

In *Mystery and Manners*, Flannery O'Connor says of the senses:

> He [the fiction writer] appeals through the senses, and you cannot appeal through the senses with abstractions.

Sight, sound, smell, touch and taste. Through the senses the writer can reach what Conrad calls "the secret springs of responsive emotion."

1. He was a man of about forty.
2. He was a high-colored gent no longer young and redolent of whiskey.

1. Jenny, dressed all in gold, crossed the room.
2. Jenny's gold slippers slapped on the parquet as the slender perfumed doll crossed the room.

1. She was a black-haired woman with bracelets on her wrists.
2. Her sleek black head nodded and her wrists were active showing off the glinting, jingling bracelets she had bought all over the world.

Sight

Sight is most commonly and extensively used in descriptive passages, and is the sense the human sensory mechanism is best at discerning: color, form, light and shadow. It is most effective when colors are vivid and form is dramatic and in action.

This is from Harold Nicolson's *Some People*:

> In the valley thus disclosed were two armored cars: there was
> a little pool beyond with some English soldiers bathing: their
> knees and forearms showed like burnt umber against the white
> of their thighs. They ran a little way toward us, cheering, wav-
> ing their topees above their tousled heads.

The burnt umber knees and forearms *prove* these English soldiers, whose desert uniforms consist of short pants and short-sleeved blouses.

Here is Joseph Conrad's archetypal African woman from *Heart of Darkness*. All is visual except the jingle of her jewelry, and the description is given in motion:

> She walked with measured steps, draped in striped and fringed
> cloths, treading the earth proudly, with a slight jingle and flash
> of barbarous ornaments. She carried her head high; her hair
> was done in the shape of a helmet; she had brass leggings to
> the knees, wire gauntlets to the elbow, a crimson spot on her

tawny cheek, innumerable necklaces of glass beads on her neck; bizarre things, charms, gifts of witch-men, that hung about her and trembled at every step.

The drama of this description is enhanced by the motion: *walked, draped, treading, flash, carried, hung* and *trembled*.

This passage from my novel *Separations* contains brilliant colors, light and shadow, all in motion. Asa Haden has awakened on a campsite high on a wall of the Grand Canyon, to watch the dawn light:

The vertical earth began to glow. Scarlet sandstone and sulky red marble became incandescent with the light, as though with inner fires, which merged with the blue cast of the air. The fantastic wrinkling of canyons and ravines, of ridges and buttresses, was struck by living fire, turning shadows blacker than black, the whole in movement, in constant change, as the light advanced and shadow retreated. . . .

The following is from *Between the Woods and the Water* by Patrick Leigh Fermor, who is one of those British travel writers so accurate and so vivid that little fiction can touch them. The book is an account of a journey by foot across Europe. This passage describes an Easter night procession in Hungary:

Not a light showed in the town except for the flames of thousands of candles stuck along the window-sills and twinkling in the hands of the waiting throng. The men were bareheaded, the women in kerchiefs, and the glow from their cupped palms reversed the daytime chiaroscuro, rimming the lines of jaw and nostril, scooping lit crescents under their brows and leaving everything beyond these bright masks drowned in shadow. Silently forested with flames, street followed street and as the front of the procession drew level everyone kneeled, only to rise to their feet again a few seconds after it had moved on. Then we were among the glimmering ranks of poplars and every now and then the solemn music broke off. When the chanting paused, the ring of the censer-chains and the sound of the butt of the Archbishop's pastoral staff on the cobbles were joined by the croaking of millions of frogs. Woken by the bells and the music, the storks of the town were floating and crossing overhead and looking down on our little string of lights as it turned uphill to the basilica again.

The visuals here are vivid: the candlelight scooped around the faces in the forest of flames, the successive kneeling and rising of the throng as the procession passes, the glimmering ranks of poplars and the wonderful network of storks, disturbed by the festivities, "floating and crossing overhead," as Fermor sums up in the conclusion of the paragraph, "hallowed the night with a spell of great beneficence and power."

Sound

Sound is a basic, much-used sense perception, like sight, and the two often work together. Above, along with the visual impressions, we hear the jingle of the censer-chain and the stamp of the archbishop's staff, the bells and music, and the croaking of the frogs.

Sound is vital in this scene from my *The Downhill Racers*, where it proves the speed at which the ski racer is travelling:

> . . . the bottom of Siberia began to rush at me. Dimly there came, through the focus of my senses, the mounting racket of ski clatter and cloth snapping, the wind numbing my face and making my teeth ache.

Here sound is combined with the feel of the numbing of the racer's face and the ache of his teeth from the cold wind of his passage.

In a similar excerpt from Mike Wilson's *Right on the Edge of Crazy*, note the flatness of the action from a lack of sensories:

> He soared off the tunnel jump, landed, and turned left, the edge of his right ski gripping the ice, his left leg skimming along beneath him. The hill fell away quickly as he entered the section known as the compression, a deep, wide hole followed by a jump. Skiing through a compression—lots of downhill courses

had them—was something like bouncing on a trampoline. You plummeted downward, using your knees as shock absorbers at the bottom, and then sprang out, weightless. The trick was to come out without going too high in the air. When the racers landed, they had to make a left turn, then a quick right; their momentum in the second turn carried them out to a long, padded fence. This was at seventy miles an hour. Some guys got close enough to the fence to touch their elbows to it. Others got closer than that.

This passage turns from action into exposition. Seventy miles an hour is merely stated. There are no sensory impressions except for "Some guys got close enough to the fence to touch their elbows to it," which, however, is stated, not proven. If a particular racer felt the electric slap of his elbow against the padding while he leaned desperately to swerve away from the fence, then this scene might have come to life.

See how many sounds and other sense perceptions Ngaio Marsh employs in this description of an early morning in British hills in this passage from *Overture to Death*:

> *The gravel crunched under his shoes* and the dim box-borders smelled friendly in a garden that was oddly remote. Familiar things seemed mysterious as if the experience of the night had made strangers of them. The field was rimmed with silver, the spinney on the far side was a company of naked trees locked in a deep sleep from which *the sound of footsteps among the dead leaves and twigs* could not awaken them. The hillside smelled of cold earth and frosty stones. As Henry climbed steeply upwards, it was as if he left the night behind him in Pen Cuckoo. On Cloudyfold, the dim shapes took on some resolute form and became rocks, bushes and posts, expectant of the day. *The clamor of faraway cock-crows rose vaguely from the valley* like the overlapping echoes of dreams, and with this sound came the human smell of wood smoke. (Emphasis added.)

Smell

It is well known that realtors will put bread or cookies to bake in the oven of the house property they are showing to a prospective buyer, not only to give that buyer a sense of hominess but to soften his business sense.

In memory, visual recall tends to fade because new visual experiences overwhelm old ones, but odor memory seems to be permanent.

Diane Ackerman writes of remembered odors in *A Natural History of the Senses*:

> Proust's lime-flower tea and madeleines, Colette's flowers, which carried her back to childhood gardens and her mother, Sido; Virginia Woolf's parade of city smells, Joyce's memory of baby urine and oilcloth, holiness and sin; Kipling's rain-damp acacia, which reminded him of home, and the complex smells of military life ("one whiff . . . is all Arabia"); Dostoyevsky's "Petersburg stench"; Coleridge's notebooks, in which he recalled that "a dunghill at a distance smells like musk, and a dead dog like elder flowers"; Flaubert's rhapsodic accounts of smelling his lover's slippers and mittens, which he kept in a desk drawer.

In Penelope Lively's *Passing On*, country people smell a city department store:

> Within, there was that rich smell of a better-class department store: an expensively achieved amalgam of perfume, out-of-season flowers, new leather and virgin fabrics.

Proust, in *Swann's Way*, uses a quintessence of odors:

> I would turn to and fro between the prayer-desk and the stamped velvet armchairs, each one always draped in its crocheted antimacassar, while the fire, baking like a pie the appetizing smells with which the air of the room was thickly clotted, which the dewy and sunny freshness of the morning had already "raised" and started to "set," puffed them and glazed them and fluted them and swelled them into an invisible though not impalpable

country cake, an immense puff-pastry, in which, barely waiting to savor the crustier, more delicate, more respectable, but also drier smells of the cupboard, the chest-of-drawers, and the patterned wall-paper, I always returned with an unconfessed gluttony to bury myself in the nondescript, resinous, dull, indigestible, and fruity smell of the flowered quilt.

And here is a rhapsody of smells, from Susan Sontag's *The Volcano Lover.* Sir William Hamilton imagines a marble goddess in the palace garden coming to life, with smell the first sense awakened in her:

She smells the sycamores and poplar trees, resinous, acrid, she can smell the tiny shit of worms, she smells the polish on soldiers' boots, and roasted chestnuts, and bacon burning, she can smell the wisteria and heliotrope and lemon trees, she can smell the rank odor of deer and wild boar fleeing the royal hounds and the three thousand beaters in the King's employ, the effusions of a couple copulating in the nearby bushes, the sweet smell of the freshly cut lawn, the smoke from the chimneys of the palace, from far away the King on his privy, she can even smell the rain-lashed erosion of the marble of which she is made. . . .

Helen Keller was deaf and blind from the age of nineteen months. Her sense of smell, consequently, was acute. Here, in "The World I Live In," she writes of the smells of young men:

In the odor of young men there is something elemental, as of fire, storm, and salt sea. It pulsates with buoyancy and desire. It suggests all the things strong and beautiful and joyous, and gives me a sense of physical happiness.

These impressions are all related as abstractions. How can we particularize them? "As I became conscious of the young men around me, their odors came to me strongly, talcum and Bay Rum, the bite of turnips, the funkiness of mushrooms, the emanations of locker rooms and bus depots, musk and perspiration, that bright purity of sweat."

With apologies to Helen Keller.

Touch and Taste

The most specific of the senses are touch and taste, for they are particular to the individual experiencing them, whereas sight, sound and smell are also available to others nearby.

This is from Mary Karr's *The Liars' Club*:

> After . . . that trip to Houston, we didn't see Mother much. She either came home from the hospital briefly in the mornings to change clothes before heading back, or she returned after we were in bed. I would wake with *her weight tilting our mattress*, her Shalimar settling over me when she leaned to kiss me and pull up the chenille bedspread, which had *a nubble like braille under my hands*. A few times, she would sit on my side of the bed all night smoking, till the yellow light started in the windows. She had a way of waving away the smoke from my face and *making a pleasant little wind* in the process. I kept my eyes closed, knowing that if I roused she'd leave, and I wanted nothing more from her on those nights than to let me lie in the mist of perfume I still wear and to imagine the shapes her Salem smoke made. . . . *I could feel through the bedspread the faint heat of her body* as she sat a few inches from where I lay, and that heat was all I needed. (Emphasis added.)

Of course, as has already been seen, sensory perceptions are best used in battery and conjunction. Here again is Harold Nicolson's *Some People*:

> . . . when I recall that night at Covent Garden, it seems almost impossible for me to disbelieve in the reality of Eugen Malone. I can see him so vividly. I can see the sharp V of his black evening waistcoat and the two coral studs above. I can see the yellow neck emerging pouched and lined from his low collar, as he strained it up and outwards like a terrapin. I can hear the crack of joints as he crossed and uncrossed his bony knees. I can hear his reedy episcopal voice: "Ah, yes, my dear lady, yes indeed." I can smell again the hot puffs of hair-wash and jasmine rising from the auditorium, the cold chalky blast from the

stage. I sat at the back of the box, tilting my chair backwards into red shadows: in the foreground the frame of the box cut across confused light, beyond it and in perspective the frame of the stage soared angular and sharply illumined: in front two heads in silhouette—the gay and youthful head of Mrs. Lintot, the mournful head of Eugen Malone.

This is the opening paragraph of Henry James's *The Wings of the Dove*:

She waited, Kate Croy, for her father to come in, but he kept her unconscionably, and there were moments at which she showed herself, in the glass over the mantel, a face positively pale with irritation that had brought her to the point of going away without sight of him. It was at this point, however, that she remained; changing her place, moving from the shabby sofa to the armchair upholstered in a glazed cloth that gave at once— she had tried it—*the sense of the slippery and the sticky. . . .* (Emphasis added.)

And slippery and sticky is her father.

Description of taste is almost always given in terms of other senses or in comparisons:

The wine tasted like liquid sunlight.

Hemingway's simile of fear tasting like copper pennies.

The hot dog tasted like manna.

The heavy, slow taste of blood.

"She spoke of fruit that tasted the way sapphires look. . . ."

(Toni Morrison, *Paradise*)

An editor at Simon & Schuster pointed out to me this paragraph from *The Snowblind Moon*, by John Byrne Cooke, as one that had caught his attention through its appeal to the senses. This is the beginning of the novel and the author is bombarding the reader with sensories to establish the reality of his fiction:

For the moment, he was content. The wind gusted snow in Hardeman's face and he could hear the hard flakes striking the skeleton branches of the willows around him in the valley bottom. On either side of the narrowing valley, snowy hillsides wooded with lodgepole pine and naked aspens rose into the soft layer of cloud that obscured the ridgetops. Saddle leather creaked as the horse shifted its weight to one hind leg and crooked the other hoof up on its toe. The sounds were clean and sharp in the cold air. Hardeman could make out the noise of two branches rubbing together twenty yards away and the rush of water over a rock in the small open patch of river nearby.

In the following passage from *Cold Mountain*, Charles Frazier is introducing his female protagonist on her farm. Here she has crept inside a boxwood hedge looking for eggs. See how many sense impressions Frazier employs to bring this person and this place to life:

She folded her skirts tightly about her legs, and on hands and knees worked her way inside the boxwood. Its branches scratched at her forearms and face and neck as she pushed forward. The ground beneath her hands was dry and littered with chicken feathers and old chicken shit and the hard dead leaves of the bush. Inside, there was a hollow place. The thick outer growth of leaves was just a husk enclosing a dim room.

Ada sat up in it and looked about on the ground and in the branches for eggs but found only a broken shell, dried yolk the color of rust in the jag-edged cup. The boxwood bower smelled of dust and of the sharpness and bitterness of chickens.

Stephen King sets a scene at the beginning of *The Dead Zone*, employing specifics and the sensories:

They were skating on a *cleared patch* of *Runaround Pond* in *Durham*. The bigger boys were playing hockey with old *taped* sticks and using a couple of *potato baskets* for goals. The little kids were just farting around the way little kids have done since time immemorial—their *ankles bowing comically in and out*,

their *breath puffing* in the frosty *twenty-degree air*. At one corner of the cleared ice *two rubber tire*s burned *sootily*. . . . (Emphasis added.)

William Styron has a large vocabulary and he uses a great many big
words in this passage from his story "Love Day" in his *A Tidewater
Morning*, but see how many sensory impressions he employs in this mar-
velous description of the launching of a ship on the James River:

And it *had* been thrilling to watch the mechanics, at once brutal
and delicate, of setting loose the behemoth into its natural element—freeing from its uterine dry dock into the strife-torn seas
the "biggest, most complex and costly moveable object made
by human hands" (my father's words). It had required nine
hours, this monstrous parturition, set into motion long before
dawn by gangs of floodlit chanting Negroes swinging oak battering rams that knocked down, at precisely timed intervals,
one after another of the score of telephone pole-sized pilings
that for months had held in equipoise thousands of tons of
inert steel. "A marvel of technology!" said my father. I was
enraptured by this sight: the sweating black figures sang in a
rhythmic chorus, wild, scary, African. It was controlled bedlam,
and it was also splendidly dangerous. Now and then a pole
would split apart nastily, or topple the wrong way, and the
Negroes would drop the ram with a thunderous noise and scatter
for their lives. . . . Their labor ended at the stroke of noon,
when two events took place almost together. First, in an act of
godlike finality, Mr. Gresham, an engineer colleague of my
father's, hunched down deep in a pit beneath the hull, pressed
a button that detonated a dynamite cap, blowing off the top of
the single upright that remained. . . . What a sight—this new
sweetheart of the seas being birthed, lubricated in its passage
down the ways by dirty masses of tallow as high as snowdrifts.
The tallow slithered out from beneath the keel in gigantic curlicues and sent afloat to the festive onlookers a smell of rancid
mutton. At nearly the same instant that Mr. Gresham pushed

his button, I heard Mrs. Herbert Hoover warble: "I christen thee *Ranger!*" I noticed that her slip was showing, and then she went *clunk* with the bottle, *clunk* again at the prow sliding away from her before she solidly connected. . . .

There is some rather exuberant phraseology here that one might question: "setting loose the behemoth," "monstrous parturition," "the strife-torn seas." But never mind, the observation and the sensories are very fine: the floodlit, chanting Negroes with the battering ram; the toppling poles; the gigantic curlicues of dirty tallow; the smell of rancid mutton; the *clunk, clunk*, as Mrs. Herbert Hoover swings the christening bottle; and the last small-scale wonderful item of her slip showing.

❧ CHAPTER 3 ❧

Words

We went for a bald style . . . profound suspicion of adjectives and making the verb do the work.
—JOHN LE CARRÉ

It was Gustave Flaubert's dictum that there is always *le mot juste*, the correct word. His famous advice to Maupassant:

> Whatever one wishes to say, there is one noun only by which to express it, one verb to give it life, one adjective only which will describe it. One must search until one has discovered them, this noun, this verb, this adjective, and never rest content with approximations, never resort to trickery, however happy, or vulgarisms, in order to dodge the difficulty.

Adjectives

Hemingway said that he had been taught by Ezra Pound to "distrust adjectives as I would later learn to distrust certain people in certain situations. . . ."

Voltaire speaks of the adjective as the enemy of the noun.

John Braine's rule is to try to do without adjectives. The English language possesses a vast store of synonyms, and to reject adjectives means the author must search this store for *le mot juste* noun.

Judith Krantz, author of *Princess Daisy*, is a potent adjectivizer. Princess

Daisy's father is "a great war hero and incomparable polo player," her mother "a matchless romantic American movie star." Surely Krantz could have searched a little more earnestly for the correct and just nouns.

But observe the power of the adjectives in this passage from Gabriel García Márquez's *The General in His Labyrinth*. General Bolivar is on his deathbed:

> He examined the room with the clairvoyance of his *last* days, and for the first time he saw the truth: the *final borrowed* bed, the *pitiful* dressing table whose *clouded, patient* mirror would not reflect his image again, the *chipped porcelain* washbasin with the water and towel and soap meant for other hands, the *heartless* speed of the *octagonal* clock racing toward the *ineluctable* appointment of seven minutes past one on his *final* afternoon of December 17. Then he crossed his arms over his chest and began to listen to the *radiant* voices of the slaves singing the six o'clock *Salve* in the mills, and through the window he saw the diamond of Venus in the sky that was dying forever, the *eternal* snows, the *new* vine whose *yellow* bellflowers he would not see bloom on the *following* Saturday in the house, closed in mourning, the *final* brilliance of life that would never, through eternity, be repeated again. (Emphasis added.)

This passage would lose most of its wonder without the repeated *final*, and the other adjectives—*pitiful, patient, heartless, ineluctable, radiant* and *eternal*—all of which give color and life to their nouns but also reenforce a larger layer of meaning.

Adjectives are strong and persuasive in this passage from James Joyce's short story "Araby":

> The *high cold empty gloomy* rooms liberated me and I went from room to room singing. From the front window I saw my companions playing below in the street. Their cries reached me *weakened and indistinct* and, leaning my forehead against the *cool* glass, I looked over at the *dark* house where she lived. (Emphasis added.)

Here is some early Hemingway:

> On the first of May at the Porte Maillot in the evening the
> crowd were trying to get back into the city through the gate.
> The Police charged the crowd and I saw from the top of a taxi-
> cab the scared, white, proud face of the nineteen year old boy
> who looked like a prep school quarter-back and had just shot
> two policemen.

Hemingway makes the following changes in revision, using a stronger
verb for the crowd's action, giving the policemen swords and removing
the commas from between his flood of adjectives, which he has apparently
not yet learned to distrust:

> I have watched the police charge the crowds with swords as
> they milled back into Paris through the Porte Maillot on the
> first of May and seen the frightened proud look on the white
> beaten up face of the sixteen year old kid who looked like a
> prep school quarter back and had just shot two policemen.

It is as though Hemingway presented those adjectives without commas
in order to make them seem fewer.

Describing his sisters, Laurie Lee unabashedly hurls adjectives at the
reader in *The Edge of Day*, and they are wonderful:

> How magnificent they appeared, full-rigged, those towering
> girls, with their flying hair and billowing blouses, their white-
> mast arms stripped for work or washing.

Adverbs

García Márquez, for his part, is distrustful of adverbs, especially in Spanish,
where they take the ending *mente*, which he deplores. As he points out
below, he seeks to use adverbs less and less often:

> Before *Chronicle of a Death Foretold*, there are many. In
> *Chronicle*, I think there is one. After that, in *Love* [*Love in the
> Time of Cholera*], there are none. In Spanish, the adverb *-mente*

is a very easy solution. But when you don't want to use *-mente* and look for another form, it is always better.

So it is with Marcia Davenport, author of the 1943 novel *The Valley of Decision*, when asked in an interview in *The New Yorker* what she might change if she were writing *The Valley of Decision* today:

> The fact that it's got so many adverbs in it. A really civilized and cultivated writer of the English language will turn inside out to avoid adverbs. When you're young, you don't realize that that's a lazy way of characterizing what someone says— "she said sadly," "gaily," "bitterly," "coldly." You shouldn't do that.

Still, one can never forget that great fish in Hemingway's *The Old Man and the Sea* leaping *unendingly* out of the ocean.

In this passage from the D.H. Lawrence short story, "Love Among the Haystacks," Lawrence employs adverbs to characterize the father and his sons, Geoffrey and Maurice, as they stack hay:

> Geoffrey waited, the blue tines of his fork glittering in expectation: the mass rose, his fork swung beneath it, there was a light clash of blades, then the hay was swept onto the stack, caught by Maurice, who placed it judiciously. One after another, the shoulders of the three men bowed and braced themselves. All wore light blue, bleached shirts, that stuck close to their backs. The father moved mechanically, his thick, rounded shoulders bending and lifting dully: he worked monotonously. Geoffrey flung away his strength. His massive shoulders swept and flung the hay extravagantly.

The following paragraph, however, is dulled by its adverbs:

> *Rapidly* shutting his eyes, grappling with the facts, he knew he had been hit. *Cautiously* opening one eye, the wide intersection seemed filled with stopped cars and people *hurriedly* stepping out of them. He sat up. Pain slid *achingly* up his left leg, as he saw the mass of blood coating his leg in a slick glistening layer.

Instinctively clutching his hands to the long wound, he *futilely* pressed the skin together to stop the bleeding.

Verbs

Notice the powerful verbs, which make adverbs unnecessary, in this action sequence from Norman Mailer's *The Naked and the Dead*:

> A machine gun lashed at him from across the river, and he ducked into his hole. In the darkness, it spat a vindictive white light like an acetylene torch, and its sound was terrifying. Croft was holding himself together by the force of his will. He pressed the trigger of his gun and it leaped and bucked under his hand. The tracers spewed wildly into the jungle on the other side of the river.

Lashed. Ducked. Spat. Leaped and bucked. Spewed. The verbs are violent because the action is violent. Even the adverb *wildly*, modifying *spewed*, may be unnecessary since *wildly* is implied by *spewed*, but *vindictive* is effective, for that is the way the white light seems to Croft, the point of view in this scene.

In an article in *The New York Review of Books*, February 4, 1999, on U.S. Grant's *Personal Memoirs*, James M. McPherson calls the book "the most revelatory autobiography of high command to exist in any language." He points out that in an era when commands to subordinates were usually written, and the lack of clear writing and consequent misunderstandings often affected the outcome of battles, the language of General Grant's was always clear and unmistakable. McPherson gives the reader these examples having to do with the battle at Champion's Hill.

To General Francis P. Blair:

> Move at early dawn toward Black River Bridge. I think you will encounter no enemy by the way. If you do, however, engage them at once.

To General John A. McClernand:

> The entire force of the enemy has crossed the Big Black. . . .

Disencumber yourself of your [supply] train, select an eligible position, and feel the enemy.

To General James B. McPherson:

Pass all trains and move forward to join McClernand with all possible dispatch.

To General William T. Sherman:

Start one of your divisions on the road with its ammunition wagons. . . . Great celerity should be shown in carrying out the movement. The fight might be brought on at any moment—we should have every man on the field.

The author goes on to say: ". . . these sentences bristle with verbs of action: move . . . engage . . . disencumber . . . select . . . feel . . . move . . . start." Grant used few adjectives and fewer adverbs and then only those necessary to enforce his meaning: "*early* dawn," "engage *at once*," "move . . . with *all possible dispatch*," "*great* celerity," "*every* man."

Consider Grant's famous reply to General Simon B. Buckner's terms for the surrender of Fort Donelson: "No terms except an unconditional and immediate surrender can be accepted. I propose to move immediately on your works." Not an excess word here; the three adjectives and single adverb strengthen and clarify the message. The words produce action—they become action. The same stylistic qualities of action verbs with active voice characterize most of the *Personal Memoirs*.

Nouns

Nouns, of course, are what and who it is all about, the very basis of everything. Regard the solidity that stems from these nouns of Michael Chabon's in his short story "Werewolves in Their Youth." Paul Kovel is bringing out of the house, to take to the dump on his mother's orders, his father's stuff. The list of effects not only characterizes the father, it forms a solid platform for the story:

I could see the fuzzy sleeve of my father's green angora sweater poking out of one carton, and, through the finger holes in the side of another, I could make out the cracked spines of his college chemistry texts. Stuffed into the spaces among the boxes and into odd nooks of the car's interior were my father's bicycle helmet, his clarinet case, his bust of Paul Morphy, his brass wall barometer, his shoeshine kit, his vaporizer, the panama hat he liked to wear at the beach, the long plastic bedpan that had come home from the hospital with him after his deviated-septum operation and now held his razors and combs and the panoply of gleaming instruments he employed to trim the hair that grew from the various features of his face, a grocery bag full of his shoe trees, his Montreal Junior Chess Championship trophy he had won in 1953, his tie rack, his earmuffs, and one Earth shoe.

Modifiers

In the following passage, each noun and verb has its modifier, which detracts instead of adding or qualifying:

> Powerfully straining his muscular arms above his head and twisting his thick torso, Jack turned swiftly away from his disorganized closet and made a quick spin on the heel of his brand new Reebok. His gray warmup pants tightened sleekly on his long, well-formed legs, and his long-sleeved sweatshirt settled comfortably around his broad back.

Patterns of modifiers, especially when doubled, create an unfortunate and sometimes ridiculous rhythm:

> Bright and early in the morning he set out for the big, new school, carrying his brown leather satchel and his heavy tin lunchbox, which he left in the dim, smelly cloakroom, and went to his stiff, little desk, where he greeted Miss Tomkins, the young, pretty teacher.

Here is Curzio Malaparte doubling his modifiers detrimentally in his novel *Kaputt*:

> I noticed his wide, flat face with its hard, coarse features. His eyes

shone with a deep black fire in his pale, earthen-colored face.

See how comfortable and effective the modifiers combine with their nouns and verbs in this beginning of "A Wine Cave in Algeciras, 1949" by Laurie Lee:

> We entered to the cry of a fisherman singing an ecstatic fandango that shivered the roots of one's hair. The singer, who was leaning against a huge sweating barrel of amontillado, was a short wiry little man, scrub-haired, swarthy-faced, with a profile from Egypt. He wore a blue jersey and torn linen trousers, and he was surrounded by a rapt group of friends whose shining weather-beaten faces were creased by the very excesses of pleasure.
>
> We drank black wine at sixpence a bottle and listened to him. He stood there stiffly, his eyes closed, his dark face raised to the light, singing with a powerful controlled passion that shook his whole body through. At the beginning of each verse his limbs convulsed, as though gathering their strength; and at the end he reached such shuddering paroxysms of intricate invention that the whole room roared with praise. He sang through his nose, with the high-pitched cry of Africa, and he sang with the most natural grief and happiness, varying his words with little phrases of his own full of sly wickedness and tragic beauty.

Here is advice from Isaac Babel:

> . . . before I take out all the rubbish, I break the text into shorter sentences. The more full stops the better. I'd like to have that passed into law. Not more than one idea and one image in one sentence. Never be afraid of full stops. . . .
>
> I take out all the participles and adverbs I can. Participles are heavy, angular, they destroy the rhythm. They grate like tanks going over rubble. Three participles to one sentence and you kill the language. All that "resenting," "obtaining," "concentrating," and so on. Adverbs are lighter. They can even lend you wings in a way. But too many make the language spineless. . . . A noun needs only one adjective, the choicest.

Only a genius can afford two adjectives to one noun. . . .

In her Booker Prize novel, *The God of Small Things*, Arundhati Roy constructs unfamiliar forms of words by jamming words together, such as *thunderdarkness, suddenshudder, soapslippery, fishswimming, oldfood smell, slushgreen paddy fields, fallingoff noises.* In an early scene a small black bat climbs up a hymnsinging woman's sari:

> The singing stopped for a "Whatisit? Whathappened?" and for
> a Furrywhirring and a Sariflapping.

I find some of these combinations to be effective; others cause me to want to argue with the author. Often the combined word will jump off the page as having more importance than it should have.

However, the inclination to discover more effective means of writing prose fiction deserves some honor.

Clichés and Junk Words

Clichés are trite phrases, hackneyed expressions, truths that have been revealed too often and have lost all freshness. Junk words should be dealt with on the theory that what does not add does detract.

Many adjectives joined to particular nouns form the bonded pairs of clichés: *frisky kittens, stately oaks, graceful porticoes, hard-bitten cops, friendly smiles.* Some are redundant as well: *doleful mourners, tall skyscrapers, innocent maidens.*

The easiest words to get rid of are the flimsy qualifiers that hardly mean anything at all and thus detract rather than add: *a little, a bit, rather, sort of, kind of, quite, very, pretty* (as in *much*), *slightly, mostly,* etc. For example: *Sort of tired = tired, pretty expensive = expensive, a bit hard = hard, kind of unhappy = unhappy.*

Very may give emphasis, but more often it merely clutters: *very majestic, very ridiculous, very gorgeous.*

Positive words are usually more effective than negative: "He is always late" is better than "He is never on time."

A reviewer complains of a novelist's vocabulary: "X uses extreme words—*vastly, violently, madly, impossibly, ghastly, heavenly, furiously*—far too often. She does the same with bland adjectives—*nice, kind, good, terrific, super.*"

Ezra Pound's advice to Ernest Hemingway was as follows:

Use no superfluous words.

Use no adjective which does not add something.

Go in fear of abstractions.

Another Warning Against Abstractions

Here is the novelist Sebastian Faulks describing a moment of revelation in the novel *Charlotte Gray*:

> Only when he heard her stunned and gasping reaction to his voice did he fully register the depth of his passion for her. There was such struggle and humility in her tone, the sense of something so long and terribly desired, that he felt crushed by it. But for the first time since he had known Charlotte he no longer felt intimidated and he understood that the complexity of her feelings was not for her the source of any sense of superiority but, on the contrary, the cause of awful anguish. For the first time he believed that his own life, however tarnished in his eyes, was what was necessary for the redemption of hers.

When the reader sees the word *redemption*, he reaches for his gun. Faulks can't get away with this wire-entanglement of abstractions: "depth of his passion," "struggle and humility," "long and terribly desired," "intimidated," "complexity," "superiority," "awful anguish," "*redemption.*" This paragraph sounds good in a highfalutin way, but it is impossible to come up with any *felt* sense out of it.

Anglo-Saxon vs. Latinate

Anglo-Saxon words are usually better than Latinate words, which are largely polysyllabic, and are more formal. Their stress is on the second syllable, such as in *transmit, conduct, resist*, while their Anglo-Saxon synonyms, *send, build* and *stop*, are single syllables. *Hearty* and *mock* are more forceful than *cordial* and *imitate*. Latinate words often turn into euphemisms for the blunter often shocking Anglo-Saxonisms: *intercourse* and *excrement*, for instance, for *fuck* and *shit*.

Overusing Latinate words produces stuffy prose. George Orwell captured the flab of Latinate English in his translation of a passage from "Ecclesiastes" into modern-day institutional Latinese:

> I returned and saw under the sun, that the race is not to the swift, nor yet riches to men of understanding, nor yet favor to men of skill, but time and chance happeneth to them all.

> Objective consideration of contemporary phenomena compels the conclusion that success or failure in competitive activities exhibits of contemporary prescriptive. . . .

Yet in the line "How weary, stale, flat and unprofitable," how wonderfully effective is the long Latinate *unprofitable* following the short Anglo-Saxon *weary, stale* and *flat*?

Joseph Conrad, the great English prose stylist, whose native language was not English, complained, as quoted by Ford Madox Ford in *Joseph Conrad: A Personal Remembrance*, that no English word is simply a word, that all English words are instruments for exciting blurred emotions:

> "Oaken" in French means "made of oak wood"—nothing more. "Oaken" in English connotes innumerable moral attributes: it will connote stolidity, resolution, honesty, blond features, relative unbreakableness, absolute unbendableness—also, made of oak. . . . The consequence is that no English word has clean edges: a reader is always, for a fraction of a second, uncertain as to which meaning of the word the writer intends. Thus, all English prose is blurred. Conrad desired to write prose of extreme limpidity. . . .

Passive Voice

> Never use the passive voice—it leads to effeminacy and homosexuality.
>
> —Colonel James Rembert, Department of English, The Citadel

The passive voice is (at least) another deadener.

A verb is *active* when its subject is performing whatever action the verb is describing. The verb is *passive* if its subject is being acted upon by something or someone else. The passive voice is composed of *is, was* or *has been*, plus a past participle:

> Horns were blown, bells were rung, ticker tape was thrown from the windows, embraces were exchanged.

> Horns blew, bells rang, ticker tape flew out the windows, couples embraced.

Would

Beware of extended use of the habitual case:

> In the morning he would leap out of bed early. He would don his boots and arm into his plaid wool shirt. He would slosh down a cup of hot coffee. Usually he would fight with his wife, then he would go outside with his shotgun.

Nothing is actually taking place before the reader, who is being *told*, not shown. These are generalized happenings, not particular ones. The habitual case is indefinite, unparticular and not specific. Unless a passage is to be very brief, it is more effective to show a particular case and imply that it is habitual.

> Buck saw no need to vary his morning routine. He snatched his shotgun off the wall, jammed some shells into his pocket, and strode outside.

Sentence Modifiers

Consider the placement of modifiers:

"Evenly, slowly, meditatively she . . ." Did what?

"The huge, black, poison-laden . . ." What?

"The nasty, muttering, pale little . . ." Who?

These modifiers are all presented before the object, person or verb. If the page had to be turned before the noun or verb, the reader would have no idea what was coming.

The particular is more vivid than the general, the specific than the abstract, so the writer tries to present the particular and the specific. The sentence modifier, which comes *after* the noun or verb, is more effective in establishing the particular and the specific than word modifiers, which *precede* the noun or verb.

1. A Siamese cat with crossed blue eyes, a crook in his tail, and a yowl when hungry that rattled the cans of Kitty-Tuna on the pantry shelf . . .
2. The cook stood beside the table, stiff as a rocket in his white cap, quivering at attention.

The following is from Walter Van Tilburg Clark's first chapter of *The Ox-Bow Incident*:

> The sky was really changing now, fast; it was coming on to storm, or I didn't know signs. Before it had been mostly sunlight, with only a few cloud shadows moving across fast in a wind that didn't get to the ground, and looking like burnt patches on the eastern hills where there was a little snow. Now it was mostly shadow, with just gleams of sunlight breaking through and shining for a moment on the men and horses in the street, making the guns and metal parts of the harness wink and lighting up the big sign on Davies' store and the sagging white veranda of the inn. And the wind was down to earth and continual, flapping the men's garments and blowing out the horses' tails like plumes. The smoke from houses where supper had been started was lining straight out to the east and flowing down, not up. It was a heavy wind with a damp, chill feel to it, like comes before snow, and strong enough so it wuthered under the arcade and sometimes whistled, the kind of wind that even now makes me think of Nevada quicker than anything else I know. Out at the end of the street, where it merged into the road to the pass, the look of the mountains had changed

too. Before they had been big and shining, so you didn't notice the clouds much. Now they were dark and crouched down, looking heavier but not nearly so high, and it was the clouds that did matter, coming up so thick and high you had to look at them instead of the mountains. And they weren't firm, spring clouds, with shapes, or the deep, blue-black kind that means a quick, hard rain, but thick, shapeless and gray-white like dense steam, shifting so rapidly and with so little outline that you more felt than saw them changing.

Everything is in action here, with the nouns, verbs and their modifiers, and the sentence modifiers supporting the action.

Here is some plain good writing from Raymond Chandler's *The Lady in the Lake*, efficiently encompassing duration, movement and menace.

Half an hour and three or four cigarettes later a door opened behind Miss Fromsett's desk and two men came out backwards, laughing. A third man held the door for them and helped them laugh. They all shook hands heartily and the two men went across the office and out. The third man dropped the grin from his face and looked as though he had never grinned in his life.

This is cinematographic writing, the writing mimicking the action: the wait marked by cigarettes, the backs coming out the door, then the laughing. The repeated *laugh* at the end of the sentence pulls the laughter through the intervening time. The sharp *out* at the end of the sentence echoes the door closing.

Assonance, Alliteration and Rhythm

In *Treasure Island*, Jim Hawkins is observing the antics of the unattended *Hispaniola*:

I was not a hundred yards from her when the wind came again in a clap, she filled on the port tack, and was off again, stooping and skimming like a swallow.

"Stooping and skimming like a swallow" is not only a lovely visual image in action, but the variations of s—st, sk and sw—in the sound effects of the *Hispaniola* sailing with no one at the helm are tonic to the ear.

The famous ending of James Joyce's story "The Dead" also employs sound repetitions:

> Yes, the newspapers were right; snow was general all over Ireland. It was falling on every part of the dark central plain, falling softly upon the Bog of Allen and, further westward, softly falling into the dark mutinous Shannon waves. It was falling, too, upon every part of the lonely churchyard where Michael Furey lay buried. It lay thickly drifted on the crooked crosses and headstones, on the spears of the little gate, on the barren thorns. His soul swooned slowly as he heard the snow falling faintly through the universe, and, faintly falling, like the descent to their last end, upon the living and the dead.

The *s*s accumulate like the snowflakes themselves, and the repetitions of "falling softly," "softly falling," "thickly drifted," "faintly falling," have a lulling effect on the reader as well as dramatizing Gabriel's sleepy mood. And the long vowel sounds throughout contribute to the somber knelling of the connection of the living and the dead.

Here are plosives, hard quick sounds that speed up the pace, from Dashiell Hammett's *Red Harvest*:

> The chief's car got away first, off with a jump that hammered our teeth together.

This is from Vladimir Nabokov's *Lolita*:

> Lolita, light of my life, fire of my loins. My sin, my soul. Lo-lee-ta: the tip of the tongue taking a trip of three steps down the palate to tap, at three, on the teeth. Lo, Lee, Ta.
>
> She was Lo, plain Lo, in the morning, standing four feet ten in one sock. She was Lola in slacks. She was Dolly at school. She was Dolores on the dotted line. But in my arms she was always Lolita.

There is a burst of alliteration in the first paragraph, *l*s and *t*s exploding in the ecstatic celebration of the name of the narrator's beloved: *light, life, loins, tip, tongue, Lo, Lee, Ta.*

In the second paragraph Nabokov repeats the long vowel sound of the *o*s in *Lo, Lola, Dolly, Dolores, Lolita.* Long vowel sounds are solemn; they signify a story of seriousness and maybe tragedy.

Accidental rhythms jerk the reader out of the progression of the prose:

> Tom ran down the last block hard and fast, and didn't pause
> until the lamppost there was passed.

But Dickens, in *A Tale of Two Cities*, is able to use rhythm to pull the reader along with him:

> There were a king with a large jaw, and a queen with a plain face, on the throne of England; there were a king with a large jaw, and a queen with a fair face, on the throne of France. In both countries it was clearer than crystal to the lords of the State preserves of loaves and fishes, that things in general were settled forever.

Repetitions

Accidental and careless word repetitions are poisonous to good prose, but thoughtful repetitions can prove very effective. Orators and preachers have always depended on repetitions and parallel constructions building to a climax, and here Dickens, in *Bleak House*, describes the death of Jo, the pathetic crossing-sweeper:

> Dead, your Majesty. Dead, my lords and gentlemen. Dead, Right Reverends and Wrong Reverends of every order. Dead, men and women, born with Heavenly compassion in your hearts. And dying thus around us every day.

Ernest Hemingway under the tutelage of Gertrude Stein ("A rose is a rose is a rose") was, in his early years, trying to construct a new American language for fiction, and he used repetitions very effectively. This is from his story "In Another Country":

> In the *fall* the war was always there, but we did not go to it any more. It was *cold* in the *fall* in Milan, and the dark came very early. Then the electric lights came on, and it was pleasant along the streets looking in the windows. There was much game hanging outside the shops, and the snow powdered in the fur of the foxes and the *wind blew* their tails. The deer hung stiff and heavy and empty, and small birds *blew* in the *wind*, and the *wind* turned their feathers. It was a *cold fall* and the *wind* came down from the mountains." (Emphasis added.)

American writers of the twentieth century have, whether they rebel against it or emulate it, been much influenced by Hemingway.

Hemingway's short sentences are a matter of personal style. So are Henry James's longer, finely balanced and qualified ones, so are Marcel Proust's even longer ones, pages long, each a miracle of structure. So are Faulkner's powerful sentences with their negative dependent qualifying clauses in parallel construction.

Simple Sentences, Compound Sentences

In the above passage from Hemingway, the sentences are mostly compound, hung together by *and*, the two parts of the sentence rather arbitrarily matched together insofar as sense is concerned, but effectively where rhythm is concerned.

In *The Grapes of Wrath*, John Steinbeck creates a biblical roll to his prose by the use of *and* to begin his sentences and by the use of the compound form as Hemingway does above:

> And after awhile the man with the guitar stood up and yawned. Good night, folks, he said.
>
> And they murmured, Good night to you.
>
> And each wished he could pick up a guitar, because it is a gracious thing. Then the people went to their beds, and the

camp was quiet. And the owls coasted overhead, and the coyotes gabbled in the distance, and into the camp skunks walked, looking for bits of food. . . .

Simple sentences may be most effective for describing action, but run-on sentences have a speeded-up, breathless quality that is effective as well. Here are examples: The first, in short sentences, is from an Apache-cavalry skirmish, from my novel *Apaches* (the cavalry is trying to capture a trouble-making Apache holy man called the Dreamer), and the second, in one long, run-on sentence, is a scene in a World War II battle from an unfinished novel titled *Homecoming*:

. . . there was fire from the canyon wall and the two troopers who had cocked their pieces were slammed out of their saddles. Others fired back, horses wheeling. Another trooper fell, yelling for help. Bunch spurred, dismounted, and helped the wounded man up behind his saddle. Cutler . . . saw Pizer spur up to where the Dreamer had risen and empty his revolver point-blank. Instantly the adjutant was flung to the ground, his chest a bloody mush. Firing back, the command followed the officers retreating up the hillside. There was a steady yelling, hoarser from the troopers, shriller from the Apaches. The firing ceased when the troops had passed out of effective range. Cutler saw four, five, six empty saddles.

From the top of the ridge the river bottom spread out below us, and it was a German river crossing in their retreat, four pontoon bridges across the river that snaked in broad curves down the valley where the snow was torn up with great muddy splashes, and what looked like the whole Kraut Army milling like wounded hyenas, soldiers and machines and artillery, a lot of it horse drawn, and dead horses spotted in the snow, and the P-51s coming down along the river with all their guns firing at the poor bastards on the pontoon bridges, plane after plane, with a flourish of wings slanting up once almost lazily and then down-slanting and faster and totally intent on the strafing.

These seem to me equally effective, although the second elicits a passing salute to Ernest Hemingway.

What works, works.

Simile

The definition of *simile* in my collegiate Webster's dictionary is "a figure of speech comparing two unlike things that is often introduced by *like* or *as* (as in *cheeks like roses*)." Thus *blue as indigo* or *transparent as glass* would not be true similes as the things compared are not unlike.

Raymond Chandler must be the most famous employer of the extravagant simile. Here is a collection from the first twenty pages of *The Big Sleep*. Chandler's protagonist, the private detective Philip Marlowe, arrives at the Sternwood mansion where he meets the dying General Sternwood in the hothouse among the orchids there. These pages include entrance doors that would have let in a troop of Indian elephants, decorative trees trimmed as carefully as poodle dogs, the general's daughter with teeth as white as fresh orange pith and as shiny as porcelain, a vestibule as warm as a slow oven, orchid stalks like the newly washed fingers of dead men, which smell as overpowering as boiling alcohol under a blanket. The general's scanty hair is like wildflowers fighting for life on a bare rock. He sniffs at Marlowe's cigarette like a terrier at a rathole. The heat makes Marlowe feel like a New England boiled dinner. The butler's back is as straight as an ironing board. A white carpet looks like a fresh fall of snow at Lake Arrowhead. A maid looks like a nice old horse that had been turned out to pasture.

These similes often make comparisons that are wildly unlike. They serve a purpose of characterization. Marlowe is educated, irreverant, not easily impressed, cynical, a bit world-weary. Moreover, the reader is interested in Marlowe because of his responses to the data he encounters.

Here are similes from the first twenty pages of Reynolds Price's novel *Kate Vaiden*: roads rough as gullies, January cold as igloos, Kate's mother nervous as a hamster, cold as scissors, rich as the caves of Peru, normal as tapwater, a face like a used bandsaw still spinning, grinning white as daylight, Frances moving through time as though the air is stiff, quiet as rocks, cinnamon hair that looks warm as bricks, tears that drag down his cheeks like white corn-syrup, pretty as babyteeth, a face white as rice.

Again the similes assist in the characterization of Kate Vaiden. They are fresh and lively as she is fresh and lively; they are also, with a couple of exceptions (cold as igloos, rich as the caves of Peru), very much a part of her own life experience. They not only move the prose along with their fresh view of the surrounding data, they move the narrative voice along, also.

Most writers have had to cudgel their brains for similes for white, since, for one thing, characters in tense situations often exhibit white faces. White as what? Surely not snow, which is worn out. Paper? Milk? Bone? Spindrift? Lace? Blind eyes? Chandler uses the pith of an orange as a simile for whiteness; Price uses *white as daylight* and *white as rice*. *White as daylight* is a lovely, homely simile, and *white as rice* is very much a part of the heroine's daily life. Frances moving through time as though the air is stiff gives the reader respect for Kate Vaiden's powers of observation and metaphysics, while Chandler's simile of the orchid stalks like dead men's fingers reminds the reader of the focus of the novel, which is a dead man.

CHAPTER 4

Symbol and Indirection

Heard melodies are sweet, but those unheard are sweeter. . . .
—JOHN KEATS, "ODE ON A GRECIAN URN"

Symbols

In James Gould Cozzens's 1957 novel, *By Love Possessed*, there is the following description of a giant oak tree. The tree is adjacent to the Lodge at the Lake where the members of the law firm that is central to the novel (including the protagonist Arthur Winner) spend weekends and holidays:

> This tree was, indeed, worth attention.
>
> Out over the edge of the terrace parapet, out over Arthur Winner on the path below, and far beyond, the big lower boughs extended. The oak stood well removed from the old lodge's rustic front; yet Judge Lowe and Mr. Woolf, not far from the door, could be said to sit under it. The trunk, a ponderous short pillar of whitish gray bark, furrowed with massive perpendicular ridges as though to show its strength, was seven feet through. The highest twigs of the broad rounded crown were ninety feet in the air. Those first low boughs, nearly horizontal, reached sideways almost as far. Some of them were thicker than a man. Mounting in intricate symmetry, lesser boughs spread out branches too many to count, lifted in hills of leaves, leaves innumerable. Even now in September, they were kept green

and lustrous by what must be a gigantic root system, boring down to the water table, searching half an acre for food. When they came to fall, those leaves would, not a few, measure eight or more inches.

Arthur Winner's idea as a boy had been that the Ponemah oak was the biggest tree in the world. . . .

Halfway through the novel the great tree is hit by lightning, ripped open with a split a man could put his arm into. The tree has been killed, in effect, by a stroke.

Why all this attention to this tree, this big tree that overshadows such a span? This is a symbolic tree. The tree represents Noah Tuttle, the grand old man of the law firm who overshadows the other members. He dies when the tree dies, and his death uncovers a financial peculation that he has been covering up, and that young Arthur Winner, who will replace him, must continue to cover up. That is the central plot of this considerable novel.

According to Webster a symbol is something common or tangible that stands for or suggests something invisible or intangible. Symbols are so commonly employed we hardly notice them. A flag is a symbol for a nation, bears or tigers for an athletic team, a dove for the Holy Spirit and so on. In the Stephen Crane story "The Bride Comes to Yellow Sky," the bride is a symbol for civilization. In *Doctor Zhivago*, the young woman Lara is the symbol of Russia in turmoil; in *The Forsyte Saga*, Irene is the art spirit; in *Moby Dick*, the white whale is a symbol for a whole lot of philosophical stuff; in my novel *The Adelita*, the eponymous character is a symbol for the ideals of revolutionary Mexico; in William Faulkner's story "The Bear," that bear is highly symbolic as well as very real.

The impulse here works like the mechanics of a joke. The joke builds to a point where the auditor must complete the implication or fill out the extrapolation. In either case this connection is not made for him. His pleasure or amusement comes from making the connection himself.

A young woman meets a fascinating man whom she admires for his speed on the tennis court. When she compliments him he says, "Yes, and

I have an artificial leg. Just step in here and I'll show you." He takes her into a room where he screws his leg off. She watches him throwing a football and compliments him, and he says, "Yes, and I have an artificial arm." He takes her into the room where he screws his arm off. He plays chess like a master, and when she compliments him on his intelligence, he says, "Yes, and I have an artificial head, just step in here . . ." Here the auditor's enjoyment comes from extrapolating what happens in the room.

When King Lear, encountering his beloved daughter Cordelia dead, says, "Pray you, undo this button," the implication is that his collar has become too tight to contain his emotion, and the emotion itself need not be mentioned.

The symbols mentioned earlier are comprehensive, book-size symbols. But authors also employ smaller workaday ones that convey meanings to characters rather than just to the reader. Here is a scene from Jane Austen's *Mansfield Park*. Fanny has a beloved older brother at home in Portsmouth, William, who has given her a chain to wear around her neck, with a little topaz cross to go with it. The two brothers at Mansfield Park, Henry, whom she does not love, and Edmund, whom she does love, have also given her chains. Henry's will not fit the holes in the cross; Edmund's will fit. This is a fine symbolic (and real) moment, the tangible chains with their intangible meanings and the probably-not-Freudian holes that do and do not fit:

> She had, to oblige Edmund, resolved to wear it [Henry's] . . .
> but it was too large for the purpose. His [Edmund's] therefore
> must be worn; and having, with delightful feelings, joined the
> chain and the cross, these memorials of the two most beloved
> of her heart, those dearest tokens so formed for each other by
> every thing real and imaginary . . . and put them around her
> neck and seen how full of William and Edmund they were . . .

When we encounter clocks in fiction, we are apt to be encountering symbols having to do with time, mortality, life span and so forth. In *The Sound and the Fury*, Quentin Compson destroys his watch hammering it with a stone. He is destroying the Southern history that is destroying him.

There is a famous symbolic clock in Thackeray's *Vanity Fair*, in old Mr. Osborne's house, where he lives with his daughters. I used this *Vanity*

Fair clock in my mystery novel *Ambrose Bierce and the Queen of Spades.* The protagonist, Tom Redmond, is in love with Amelia Brittain. She is a rich young woman with a social position; he is a poor young man without. Their relationship is much dependent upon the fact that both are great readers of novels. I have used Thackeray here as a means for Amelia to tell Tom she must marry for money and social position:

"Do you remember the clock in *Vanity Fair?*" Amelia asked.

I sipped iced tea. "Remind me."

"In the Osbornes' house there was a clock decorated with a brass grouping depicting the sacrifice of Iphigenia."

"Sacrificed so the Greek fleet could set sail against Troy," I said, to prove I knew my mythology.

"The daughter of Agamemnon," Amelia said. It was as though she was assisting me with answers to the questions of an examination. "Because the winds were blowing the wrong way, preventing the fleet from sailing."

"In the novel the clock is tolling, Mr. Osborne is wearing a kind of military suiting, brass buttons and so on. Something is wrong. The daughters ask what is wrong. And one of them says, 'The funds must be falling.' "

I didn't remember.

"The winds were unfriendly," Amelia said, watching me. "One of the daughters would have to be sacrificed."

I was irritated that she should have read more into *Vanity Fair* than I had.

"Sacrificed?" I said.

"To a marriage for economic reasons. A girl's girlhood ended before she is ready for it, because the funds are falling."

She looked disappointed because I had had to be prompted.

I could feel my heart beating. "And the funds are falling?"

She plucked up her damp, glistening tumbler and cooled her cheek with it. She nodded.

Amelia is going to have to marry a banker twice her age because the value of her father's mining stocks has deteriorated.

Why is it better to develop this scene in indirection, by implication and extrapolation, rather than in directness? Consider an example of the latter:

> "I have to marry this rich dude," Amelia said. "Do you know why?"
>
> "Why?" I said, gripping my iced tea glass.
>
> "Because Daddy's mining stocks have gone down like a stone."

"Heard melodies are sweet, but those unheard are sweeter. . . ." The hint is stronger than the flat statement. In the first instance, the reader has to contribute some thought to addressing the situation, and so becomes emotionally involved. In the second format, there is no impetus to involvement.

The following is from an unfinished novel, *Homecoming*. The protagonist, Daltrey, is a soldier in World War II:

> There wasn't any specific moment when the Battle of the Bulge was over, just one day an engineer bunch appeared with water trucks and showers, and we showered and then were furnished with new uniforms to climb into, longjohns, pants and blouses and overcoats, and even caps, no boots. When I finally took my old clothes off I found that my hair had grown into the knit cap worn inside my helmet liner. . . .

His hair having grown into the knitting of his helmet liner seems to me a good device for dramatizing the duration and the intensity of the Battle of the Bulge by indirection.

Epiphany

Epiphany refers to a divine or profane manifestation, a "showing forth." The term as a literary function was established by James Joyce, who used this device in many of the classic short stories in *Dubliners*. Gabriel's realization of his wife's involvement with the memory of the dead Michael Furey at the end of "The Dead" is an epiphany, so is the end of "Araby" (the epiphany has been underlined):

I lingered before her stall, though I knew my stay was useless, to make my interest in her wares seem the more real. Then I turned away slowly and walked down the middle of the bazaar. I allowed the two pennies to fall against the sixpence in my pocket. I heard a voice call from one end of the galley that the light was out. The upper part of the hall was now completely dark.

    <u>Gazing up into the darkness I saw myself as a creature driven and derided by vanity; and my eyes burned with anguish and anger.</u>

In Richard Ford's *Independence Day*, the protagonist-father comes to visit his ex-wife, now married to another man. He happens to observe his daughter, of whom the ex-wife has custody, giving the two of them the finger. That is also an epiphany.

Objective Correlative

Another form of indirection, objective correlative is defined by T.S. Eliot as "a set of objects, a situation, a chain of events which shall be the formula for [a] *particular* emotion."

    In Jane Austen's *Mansfield Park*, she expresses human warmth in terms of the objective correlative of a fire in the fireplace. Fanny's uncle by marriage is Sir Thomas Bertram: an aunt who also lives at Mansfield Park is Mrs. Norris. Sir Thomas's warmth is expressed by the fire he orders built in his poor-relation niece's room each day; Mrs. Norris's lack of it, by the fact that she tries to extinguish the fire:

> She was struck, quite struck, when on returning from her walk, and going into the east room again, the first thing that caught her eye was the fire lighted and burning. A fire! It seemed too much, just at that time to be giving her such an indulgence was exciting, even painful gratitude. She wondered that Sir Thomas could have leisure to think of such a trifle again, but she soon found, from the voluntary information of the housemaid, who

came in to attend it, that so it was to be every day. Sir Thomas had given orders for it.

And late in the novel:

> . . . as long as she could be safe from the notice of her aunt Norris, who was entirely taken up at first in fresh arranging and injuring the noble fire which the butler had prepared.

In the beginning of John Galsworthy's *The Forsyte Saga*, the Forsytes, a very straitlaced upper-middle-class family in London about 1887, disapprove thoroughly of Philip Bosinney, an architect. His hat becomes the objective correlative of their disapproval and disconnection from the whole spirit of art symbolized by the mutual attraction of Bosinney and Irene, the wife of one of the Forsytes:

> A story was undoubtedly told that he had paid his duty call to Aunts Ann, Juley and Hester, in a soft grey hat—a soft grey hat, not even a new one—a dusty thing with a shapeless crown.
>
> "So extraordinary, my dear—so odd!" Aunt Hester, passing through the little, dark hall (she was rather short-sighted), had tried to "shoo" it off a chair, taking it for a strange, disreputable cat—Tommy had such disgraceful friends! She was disturbed when it did not move.

Negative Space

When we look at a page from Henry James, or the Victorian novelists, or Marcel Proust, we do not see much negative, that is, open, space. The pages are dense and insistent with print. Historically, open space began to come in with dialogue set off in paragraphs, more when novelists were required to submit sufficient text to fill the two- and three-decker novels demanded by the lending libraries, which were the arbiters of literary form at the time, in order to produce more book-rental income. Novelists then employed shorter chapters, with negative space devoted to chapter heads and ends, and in general sought to open up those solid blocks of print in order to fill the three volumes with less creative effort.

Now space breaks, or line breaks as they are called by copy editors, are an integral part of the fictional page, and the spaces are indirections, often implications, or bridges over action the author has thought it better to leave to the reader's imagination.

Time is passed in a space break:

> On his fourteenth birthday, Ramon, carrying his violin in its case, was introduced to Professor Alessandro at the Conservatory.
> (space break)
> Ten years later as he stood on the stage at Madison Square Garden . . .

A sexual encounter with all its clichéd biological detail can be set off-stage by a space break:

> When he kissed her she sighed, and lay back; her limbs felt like jelly.
> (space break)
> Later, buckling his belt, he . . .

See how Norman Mailer uses space breaks in this passage between the murderer Gary Gilmore and his girlfriend, Nicole, from *The Executioner's Song*:

> He finally asked her what she'd been doing. I, Nicole said, have been sitting on my ass over at my mother's. I didn't have enough gas to come back, so I had to stay there all the goddam day. "Yes," she told him. "I've been sitting on my ass." Well, he told her, something feels different in the house than when I left this morning. Were you back here today?
>
> Yeah, I got back here today, she answered. I thought you were sitting on your ass over at your mother's all day, he said. She gave a smile and said, That's exactly what I said.
>
> Gary walked over from the car, looking as casual as if he was

going into the house, and when he passed, he slapped her front-handed across the face. Pretty sneaky. Her head was ringing like an alarm clock.

The Executioner's Song consists of short paragraphs separated by space breaks. The silence, the pauses, filled with implication and subtext, between these short, complete-in-themselves but ongoing-at-the-same-time paragraphs, is very effective.

❧ CHAPTER 5 ❧

Dialogue

Suit the action to the word, the word to the action.

—WILLIAM SHAKESPEARE, *THE TRAGEDY OF HAMLET, PRINCE OF DENMARK*

Since Sir Walter Scott, dialogue has been of vital importance to fiction. It is a primary method of revealing character. It is an integral part of scene. It is action. Dialogue should express character, advance the plot and record pertinent information, and it must do these while appearing totally realistic. It must give the impression that it is a transcription of live speech.

It is not such a transcription at all; it is very much the product of conscious craft.

Here is live speech, from the Nixon tapes. Colson's men have bungled their historic break-in of the Democratic National Committee headquarters at Watergate, and Nixon suggests that Chuck Colson organize a parallel break-in of the Republican National Committee headquarters, thereby creating the public impression of tit-for-tat. This would put Robert Dole, the Republican party chairman, in a position to sue the Democrats, as Democratic chairman Lawrence O'Brien was suing the Republicans:

NIXON: What would you think if that happened?

COLSON: I think it would be very helpful if they came in one morning and found files strewn all over the place.

NIXON: And some missing, I mean something could be very open, I mean demolished. Three or four thousand dollars worth of damage.

COLSON: That would have a very good effect.

NIXON: Right there in their convention.

COLSON: During theirs? During ours?

NIXON: Theirs. Next week.

COLSON: And then Dole is in a perfect position to say . . .

NIXON: Sue . . . sue the committee. I'd sue 'em. But what I meant is . . . it should be . . . where it's really torn up.

In *For Love and Money*, Jonathan Raban has this to say about recorded real speech:

> Literal transcriptions of tape-recorded speech may be accurate in the legal sense, but they are curiously lifeless. Shorn of gesture, emphasis, timbre and cadence, they are empty husks of what was once real conversation. Often, they make their speakers sound completely half-witted. What was said with an ironic twist of the voice now reads as a solemn pontification, what was said with intense seriousness comes out as a passing aside. Read almost any newspaper interview, and you'll conclude that the dialogue of real people is more stilted and implausible than the dialogue of invented characters. Trying to make real people sound real on the page is necessarily an exercize in impressionism. Nothing teaches one the subtleties of punctuation so well as an attempt to take a skein of actual speech and restore to it the pauses, ellipses, switches of tone and speed, that it had in life. . . . You isolate the speaker's tics and tricks of speech, his keywords, and make him say them slightly more often than he did in fact; you give him small bits of stage business to mark his silences; you invent lines of dialogue for yourself to break up a paragraph of solid talk that looks to be too long to be believable. You are trespassing, perhaps, into writing fiction, but the fiction will be truer to the man and the occasion than the literal transcription.

The playwright David Mamet, the acknowledged master of contemporary American dialogue, tries here to give the sense of the breaks and pauses of real speech, as in Nixon's last lines above:

BOB: . . . That's their way. That's their way. That's their swinish, selfish—

goddam them. What *treachery* have they not done, in the name of . . .

JOLLY: . . . I know . . .

BOB: . . . of "honesty," God *damn* them. And always "telling" us
we . . .

JOLLY: . . . yes.

BOB: . . . we were the bad ones.

But these breaks and pauses and talking on top of one another are for the ear, not the eye, and this does not work well on the printed page.

A good rule of dialogue: one thought at a time, and keep the lines short. The following is from my novel in progress, *Homecoming*. My protagonist, Daltrey, has met his old English professor in Paris just after the war. Daltrey is a sergeant, Professor Chapman a major:

> "Daltrey," Major Chapman said. "What has happened to your determination to become a writer?"
>
> "I got a letter from the editor of *Black Mask* saying he would help me get published there, if I wanted to work with him."
>
> "Ah!" the major said solemnly, sipping coffee. He was squinting at me with what I thought he must think a steely gaze. "And have you in fact been published in *Black Mask*? I am interested, of course, in the literary progress of my former students."
>
> "Well, sir, just about the time I got the letter from this editor I'd started reading Faulkner. 'The Bear' in particular."
>
> He raised one arm in a kind of Roman salute, as though calling for silence. "Oh, my goodness, yes! 'The Bear.' That grand exploration of man and nature and slavery. That most amazing southern genius, Faulkner! Daltrey, it is the first requisite of the writer that he know exactly what he should read at any given moment in his career. May I take some small credit for inducing this act of writerly intelligence?"
>
> My face felt like drying cement as I tried to grin at him.
>
> He leaned forward toward me. "So 'The Bear' was the end of your private eye ambitions!"

I was irritated by his contempt for private eye pulp fiction, and I didn't want him taking credit for turning me literary.

"Well, sir," I said. "I have been kind of busy with the war."

"And has the war provided material for your war novel?"

"The liberation of Mauthausen for one thing. For my war novel."

"Ah."

"I saw one of the lampshades."

"*Ah!*" he said explosively.

One thought to one speech and no more than, say, three sentences without notifying the reader, by some device, that it is going to be a speech and of importance. Thus, preceding Major Chapman's longish speech above, he raises his arm in a kind of Roman salute to fix the reader's attention. Here's another example:

"I will tell you the truth and the whole truth!" Big Barney cried. His knuckles were white, where he gripped the rail.

I have used speech tags above when I felt them necessary, and I do not hesitate to use the adverbs modifying speech that Marcia Davenport so decries, when I think they are useful.

In the following passage the lines of dialogue can be moved more swiftly by pruning inessentials (cuts indicated by brackets):

Jack read the news item, his brows contracted over his nose. He handed it back. "Jesus," he said.

"They executed him!" Dorothy said. ["They murdered him."]

"Possession of cocaine is a felony. [I guess you can shoot a felon trying to escape.]"

"Jack!" she cried, clutching the sheet of newsprint. "Where did you get that last stuff? [Who'd you buy it from?]"

The same thought had occurred to him. "The Fellowship," he said.

"[We're next! They've probably been watching us!] They

must know we bought some from them. Jack, let's flush it down the john! [Let's get rid of it!]"

He held up a hand, palm toward her. "[We can't panic.] They wouldn't come here for just the two of us, they'd wait for a bunch of people."

"There's a bunch of people here every night! You know they've been watching every move we make. [Everybody's watching. The neighbors're watching.] They must've known for a long time we—"

"[We can't let them run our lives,] Dottie! If we let them ruin it every time we take a snort, they've won. [We can't let them win like that!]"

Dialogue and Information

Dialogue can convey information dramatically, and thus more effectively than exposition, but dialogue devised purely for that purpose will not sound natural, with characters telling each other what each already knows, too obviously for the benefit of the reader:

"What's Jenny doing?"
"Your daughter is reading to Mrs. Benjamin, as you know she does every afternoon."
"Where's Marjorie then?"
"Your wife is at the dog pound looking over the new crop of strays."
"And Joanna?"
"Your sister Joanna, or your niece?"
Etc.

In the film *Casablanca*, the wife pleads with her husband, "Oh, Victor, please don't go to the underground meeting tonight." The wife would actually have said, "Please don't go!" or some such; the "underground meeting" is for the audience's benefit and is expository writing.

In the following passage from my short story "casus belli," each character is telling the other what he already knows, and for the reader's benefit,
but the exchange is believable in the heat of argument:

> "Ralph, you have proved on that quarter section," Blaine said
> in his high, short-of-breath voice. "It is good land. You have
> worked hard."
>
> "Well, you just write a letter to the *Cheyenne Sun* how they
> have run off another homesteader. And how it is a crime four
> or five big outfits can hold the Sweetwater for seventy miles.
> I can't bring Jessie out here, Jim."

In the following passage from my novel *Separations*, Buchanan is the
super of an exploration of the Grand Canyon of the Colorado, Daggett is
his boss and organizer of the river expedition. Buchanan is the point of
view here, as Daggett explains some history to men who probably know
it already, and to the reader, but Daggett is the kind of man who would
persist in his history lesson anyway:

> "Daggett beckoned the crew to him with some vigorous arm
> waving, pacing under the canopy. Buchanan was pleased to let
> him take over the pacing, which he'd been doing for ten days.
>
> "Some of you know the history of this grand River," Daggett
> said, when they had all assembled. "First man down was a
> horse thief name of White. Showed up at Callville on a raft,
> raving out of his head, didn't even know for sure where he'd
> put in. Said Injuns kilt his partner, so he flung a couple of
> timbers together and went on the float. Cataracts! Wild waves!
> We'll see 'em all, boys!" He shared his grin around, like bonus
> pay.
>
> "Then Major Powell and his bunch. This young fellow, Mr.
> Haden, is the historian of the outfit. He can tell you about Major
> Powell's exploration."
>
> Blushing at the attention, the college boy took off his fancy
> hat and held it in his two hands.
>
> Daggett wasn't about to let anyone else speak, however,

"That was eleven years ago," he went on. "They came down from Green River City in Wyoming, took them three months. Loads of trouble. Short of food! Upsets! Some fellows was run off. Killed by Injuns!"

Daggett paced some more, swiping at his face with his blue bandanna. "The Major made a second trip two years later," he said. "As far down the Canyon as Kanab Creek. Pat Morphy was along on that jaunt." He waggled a hand at the big boatman.

This passage allows the author to bring the reader pertinent information on the history of exploration of the Grand Canyon dramatized by a "voice," to reveal the time frame, to accomplish some characterization and to set up suspense in the danger from hostile Indians.

Junk Words in Dialogue

The following words have no use but to establish a vague sense of authenticity, but they set up an irritating pause to each line before the real dialogue begins:

"Oh, Fred, have you been to town yet?"
"Well, Anna, I just haven't got around to it."
"Uh, I was hoping—"
"Say, how about laying off me for once?"

In his recollection of his collaborations with Conrad, *Joseph Conrad: A Personal Remembrance*, Ford Madox Ford has this to say under the heading "Conversations":

One unalterable rule that we had for the rendering of conversations—for genuine conversations that are an exchange of thought, not interrogatories or statements of fact—was that no speech of one character should ever answer the speech that goes before it. This is almost invariably the case in real life when few people listen, because they are always preparing their own speeches. . . .

Conrad and Ford's edict was that a character would answer a question put four speeches before it. If this kind of formula is followed, the passages of dialogue have to be very long to accommodate questions and answers. Another way of looking at this matter is that many questions need not be answered at all in dialogue, because the answer can be inferred by the reader, in gestures, nods or speeches left out because they are not important enough to record; for example:

"Are you ready to tell your Christmas story tonight?"
"I practiced real hard!"

"How are you getting into town, Jim?"
Jim presented his thumb. "See you tonight, OK?"

"How did you do on the Calculus exam, Fred?"
Fred patted a yawn. "That's a pretty dress, Pat."

Charles Portis, in *Gringos*, employs "stripped" dialogue, without speech tags:

I followed him across the street to the little park. The old man was in bad shape. His plum face had gone off to the color of lead.
"Where in the world have you been?" he said. "I need to talk to you. Big news. You never seem to come to see me anymore."
"I've been to your house three times since Nan died."
"What, I was out?"
"Mrs. Blaney said you couldn't be interrupted. I finally got the message."
"Lucille told you that? Well, things have been all balled up lately. Look here, I want you to come by Izmal for lunch at two. Can you do that? It's important."
"Have you cleared this with Mrs. Blaney?"
"I believe you're sulking. A fancied slight? Let me tell you frankly, it's not very becoming. The poor woman made a mistake, that's all."
"Did you hear about Dr. Ritchie?"

"Yes, I did. Too bad."

"It was his heart, I think. I was there. A bad business. He was quite a man in his field, wasn't he?"

"Ritchie was adequate. Undistinguished."

Portis uses no speech tags even when there is danger of confusion as to who is speaking. There is no confusion when the characters speak lines that concern them personally, but as soon as the idea of the death of Dr. Ritchie comes up, there is a moment when the reader is uncertain of who is the speaker. This seems to me not worth risking. Stripped dialogue is not the ultimate be-all and end-all of concision. The word *said* is as innocuous as punctuation. A seasoning of speech tags would alleviate the following confusion, for instance:

"I say she's no good. She deserved what she got!"

"Frank, don't say that!"

"I said it and I meant it, Mary!"

"I hate your rotten guts, you bastard!"

"You're as bad as Mary! Why don't you go home?"

"Oh, Frank, please don't talk like that! He doesn't mean it, George."

"He means it all right, Mom!"

The reader can figure out with considerable effort who is speaking here but resents being put to the trouble.

Compare the following:

"We're going to San Diego for Christmas," Frank said. "I hope you can come, Mom."

"I just don't know," Mrs. Newman said. "It would be the first time I've gone anywhere without Daddy, you know."

"That's just sentimental and morbid, Mom," Mary said.

"Oh, I just can't make up my mind."

George leaned back in his chair with both hands cocked and forefingers pointed at her. "Better come!"

Mrs. Newman gazed around at her children with misty eyes. "Well, all right, then; I will!"

The speakers above are made perfectly clear by the speech tags. Who said what can be left out, as in Mrs. Newman's second speech, where it is clear who is speaking, without a tag, and on other occasions, such as George's speech, where he is identified in action. If this conversation were to continue, other occasions would occur where speakers could be identified by action, stage business or thought, but clarity is more important than variation.

He and *she*, when sufficient to identify the speaker, are less obtrusive than proper names, which take on a repetitive quality that can be irritating, as in the British Mysteries on TV, where Inspector Morse calls Sergeant Lewis by name in each speech addressed to him. It should be remembered that two speakers do not refer to each other by name unless some emphasis is intended.

A proper name at the end of a speech tends to sound plaintive or indecisive. Coming at the beginning it will seem forceful or imperative:

"Come with me, Mary!"
"Frank, you know you have to go by yourself!"
"You come, then, George."
"Frank, you can go to hell!"

A great deal of information, description and action can be stuffed into the stage directions accompanying a speech tag:

"I think it's wonderful that Mom's coming to San Diego with us," Frank said, cutting the deck and beginning to deal.

"She has to start getting out of the house some time," Mary said, scooping up her four cards.

George lit a cigarette and dropped the still-flaming match into the glass ashtray of the little smoking stand beside his chair. "She'll be okay," he said.

Frank waved a hand at George's cigarette smoke, which drifted up toward the open clerestory window, outside of which the palm fronds lurched and flicked in the breeze off the Bay. "Mom hates cigarettes," he said.

Holding up her cards and sorting them with her red lacquered fingernails, Mary said, "Well, Daddy died of emphysema. And so will you, Georgie."

The trim white cylinder smoking at the corner of his mouth, eyes slitted against the smoke, George picked up his hand.

"I think I will die of love," he said.

Employing variations of speech tags is *not* a way to ensure against monotony in passages of dialogue:

"If you think you're getting out of here before Tuesday, forget it," she grinned.

"I'm leaving on Monday," he argued.

"Don't think of leaving before you see the medic," she counseled.

"Well, OK, Tuesday," he conceded.

The last three speech verbs, *argued*, *counseled* and *conceded*, are all redundant.

Adverbs modifying speech tags are also often redundant and more often unnecessary. If strong speech tags and/or strong adverbs are used, the way the speech is spoken may seem more important than the speech itself:

"Do you know what a gambit is?" Mary asked unexpectedly.

"It's a sacrifice in chess," Frank said disinterestedly, glancing out at the Bay.

"It happens in life too," Mary said, leaning forward intensely.

"What's all this about?" George asked wearily.

"It's about Jesus!" Mary said happily.

To every verb its adverb.

Henry James often constructed a passage of dialogue around a repeated word, phrase or sentence that acted as a kind of armature for the speeches. This passage is from *The Wings of the Dove* and involves Kate Croy and Merton Densher; the subject is Kate's father. Notice first the linkage of *objection*, then of *escape*, finally of *turning back*:

". . . He would make himself delightful to you."

"Even while *objecting* to me?"

"Well, he likes to please," the girl explained . . . "I've seen it make him wonderful. He would appreciate you and be clever with you. It's to *me* he *objects*—that is as to my liking you."

"Heaven be praised then," cried Densher, "that you like me enough for the *objection*!"

But she met it after an instant with some inconsequence, "I don't. I offered to give you up, if necessary, to go to him. But it made no difference, and that's what I mean," she pursued, "by his declining me on any terms. The point is, you see, that I don't *escape*."

Densher wondered, "But if you didn't wish to *escape me*?"

"I wished to *escape* Aunt Maud. But he insists that it's through her and through her only that I may help him; just as Marian insists that it is through her, and through her only, that I can help *her*. That's what I mean," she again explained, "by their *turning me back*."

The young man thought. "Your sister *turns you back* too?" (Emphasis added.)

Dialect

Phonetic spelling is a crude device for indicating dialect peculiarities and, if used at all, should be employed sparingly. Misspelled words tend to assume undue importance, and the apostrophes indicating missing letters join quotation marks in constructing a barbed wire entanglement around the dialogue. The following passage from Stephen Crane's *The Red Badge of Courage* is all but unreadable:

> I see a feller git hit plum in th' head when my reg'ment was a-standin' at ease onct. An' everybody yelled out t' 'im: "Hurt, John? Are yeh hurt much?" "No," ses he. He looked kinder surprized an' he went on tellin' 'em how he felt. He sed he didn't feel nothin'. But, by dad, th' first thing that feller known

he was dead. Yes, he was. Dead—stone dead. So, yeh wanta watch out.

If the author is going to indulge in this many weird spellings and word contractions, why stop here? Why isn't *everybody* contracted, or *didn't*?

And consider this from Henry Roth's *Call It Sleep*, a much-praised novel of New York immigrant life published in 1934:

> "He didn' say it!" they jeered.
>
> "Sca'cat w'yntcha say it?" Sidney rebuked him.
>
> "I couldn't," he grinned apologetically. "He wuz stannin' dere awreddy."

This may be accurate, but it is tough on the reader.

How much cleaner the following speech looks, with no apostrophes, *g*s and *d*s merely omitted, and a minimum of phonetic spelling. It's from John Kennedy Toole's *A Confederacy of Dunces*:

> Jones looked at the old man through his sunglasses and said, "You tryna sell me another beer, a poor color boy bustin his ass for twenny dollar a week? I think it about time you gimme a free beer with all the money you make sellin pickle meat and sof drink to po color peoples. You sen you boy to college with the money you been makin in here."

Here is Faulkner in *Light in August*. Lena Grove, pregnant and searching for her baby's father, Lucas Burch, has walked from Alabama to Mississippi. In the few lines of dialogue she is given, the reader understands that she is a countrywoman and speaks like one:

> "I have come from Alabama: a fur piece. All the way from Alabama a-walking. A fur piece."

And:

> "I was trying to get up the road a pieceways before dark."

And:

> "I wouldn't be beholden," she says. "I wouldn't trouble."

Faulkner uses only one misspelling, that of *fur*. In each of the other speeches, he uses one unfamiliar word to set the tone of her speech: *pieceways*, and *beholden*. Thus when there is a longish speech by Lena, Faulkner has already shown that she speaks as a countrywoman would and does not need to labor it further:

> "Like as not, he already sent me the word and it got lost on the way. It's a far piece from here to Alabama even, and I ain't to Jefferson yet. I told him I would not expect him to write, being as he ain't any hand for letters. 'You just send me your mouthword when you are ready for me,' I told him, 'I'll be waiting.' It worried me a little at first, because my name wasn't Burch yet and my brother and his folks not knowing Lucas as well as I knew him."

Here Faulkner has not even changed the spelling of *far* and the only unfamiliar word is *mouthword*. Lena's speech is perfectly normal, but the reader has come to understand that the recorded words and spellings are not the ones she actually employs.

In this speech from a piece on a return to Ireland, "The Road to Balbriggan" by Janis Cook Newman, in the *San Francisco Chronicle* of March 15, 1998, the author has rung the sound of Irish speech perfectly by word and phrase selection, and sheer garrulousness:

> "What you'll be wanting is the road that bends and leads off the main road, past the video store where the wall is painted a yellow-gold like sun shining and sends you down past the old factory, where there's been no work for a good long time now, to the butcher shop on the corner where the Benson & Hedges advert's been painted over the old kiln bricks."

Archaic Language

Similar decisions must be made by writers trying to give the *impression* of archaic speech in a historical context. How far to go? A neutral flavor, but with an archaic or classical rhythm to enable the reader to do the work? Beware of *prithee*, *forsooth* and the like.

Here follows a fine sequence of dialogue from Charles Frazier's *Cold Mountain*, which is set in backcountry North Carolina during the Civil War. Inman, the protagonist, a deserter from the Confederate Army, encounters in the darkness a man leading a horse laden with a white bundle. When the man starts to take the bundle from the horse to drop it over a cliff, Inman sees that he is lugging an unconscious woman. Inman takes out his pistol and hits the man on the head with it. The following conversation ensues:

—I accept the merit of that.

—You merit killing, Inman said. . . .

—Don't kill me. I'm a man of God, the man said.

—Some say we all are, Inman said.

—A preacher is what I mean, the man said. I'm a preacher. . . .

—Is she dead? Inman said.

—No.

—What's the matter with her? Inman said.

—Not much. She's somewhat with child. That and what I gave her.

—What would that be?

—A little packet of powders that I bought off a peddler. He said it would put a man to sleep for four hours. It's been about half that since I dosed her up.

—And you're the daddy.

—Apparently.

—Not married to her, I reckon?

—No . . .

—How did it come to pass?

—In the normal way. A certain look of eye, bend of voice, brush of hand passing the chicken when we had dinners on the ground following Sunday services . . .

—I now believe that when I took to preaching I answered a false call.

—Yes, Inman said. I'd say you're ill-suited for that business.

This is dialogue in the continental style, which uses an initial dash rather than quotation marks. The speeches are convincing in their archaic rhythms. The reader is persuaded that this is the way men talked in North Carolina in the 1860s.

Often, however, historical novel dialogue usage tends to use a very plain diction, with some contemporary words, as in these speeches from Thomas Keneally's *Blood Red, Sister Rose*, which is set in France at the time of Joan of Arc. Keneally chooses to present his dialogue as in a play:

TANGUY: Are you serious this time? Or still farting around?

NAVAILLES: Does five o'clock suit the dauphin?

TANGUY: Five o'clock. You've had all bloody day.

NAVAILLES: Five o'clock's the best we can offer now. You'd better go and dress Charlie.

In the following passage from José Saramago's *The Gospel According to Jesus Christ*, the diction is utterly devoid of either the archaic or the contemporary. Here Jesus is in conversation with his mother and his brother James, and has just announced that he has spoken with God. Jesus and James carry on a dialogue; Mary participates at the end of the passage:

> And what did the Lord say to you, where did you see Him, and were you asleep or keeping watch. I was in the desert looking for a stray sheep when He called out to me. Are you allowed to tell us what He said. That one day He will ask for my life. All lives belong to the Lord. That's what I told Him. What did He say. That in exchange for the life I must give Him, I will have power and glory. You will have power and glory after you die, asked Mary, unable to believe her ears. Yes, Mother. . . .

This is down-to-earth normal discourse (given the subject matter). What is also of interest is that there are no question marks and no paragraphing. The lines of dialogue run serially with Mary's thoughts included. There is, however, no confusion as to who is speaking, and, in fact, the lines have a rapidly delivered quality as though they come hard on each other with no pauses.

The following is from Saramago's *The Tale of the Unknown Island*. The man and the woman are aboard the boat, which is the king's gift. The woman has already inspected it but the man has not, and the two are engaged in conversation. There is no paragraphing or internal periods, only commas with a change of speakers denoted by capitalization. Unnecessary commas and question marks have been dispensed with. Again, who is speaking is perfectly clear:

> The man said, Let's leave the philosophizing to the king's philosopher, that's what they pay him for after all, and let's eat, but the woman did not agree, First, you've got to inspect your boat, you've only seen it from the outside, What sort of state did you find it in, Well, some of the seams on the sails need reenforcing, Did you go down into the hold, has the ship let in much water, There's a bit in the bottom, sloshing about with the ballast, but that seems normal, it's good for the boat, How did you learn these things, I just did, But how, The same way you told the harbormaster that you would learn to sail, at sea, We're not at sea yet, We're on the water though, My belief was that, with sailing, there are only two true teachers, one is the sea and the other the boat, And the sky, you're forgetting the sky, The winds, The clouds, The sky, Yes, the sky.

Saramago has his own theories of punctuation, especially in dialogue. The following is translated from Portuguese by Katherine Vaz:

> When we speak, we don't use punctuation signs. . . . We speak as if we're composing music, with sounds and pauses; music is all made up of sounds and pauses and so is our speech. Expression comes from the organs of sound, and in the case of oral communication, done in person, we depend upon gestures, eye expression, the suspension of the voice, the manner in which the voice vibrates, all those things.
>
> If we speak to one another we're able to communicate so easily, without punctuation signs but with a certain music—we do when we ask, "Are you coming to my house tomorrow?" . . . What sense does it make, then, to write in a book, "So-and-so arrived and said . . ." and next to it a colon and a dash? When we speak there is no colon and no dash.

I do use commas and periods, but rather than being punctuation signs, I think of them as pause signs, in the musical sense. They signal to the reader that here he or she should make a short pause, there a longer one.

Foreign Speech

Problems similar to establishing dialect or archaic speech occur also when foreign phrases are employed, or foreign speech translated. Clarity can often come simply from surrounding context, but a usual solution is simply repeating the phrase in English, as in this exchange from Hemingway's *For Whom the Bell Tolls*:

> "Back to the palace of Pablo," Robert Jordan said to Anselmo. It sounded wonderful in Spanish.
>
> "El Palacio del Miedo," Anselmo said. "The Palace of Fear."

Focusing Dialogue

In this passage from his biography, *Ernest Hemingway: A Life Story*, Carlos Baker relates this incident when Hemingway was recuperating from his wounds in an Italian hospital:

> Agnes returned from Florence in mid-November, bringing with her an ARC nurse named Elsie Jessup, who had been granted a period of sick leave. Miss Jessup was blonde, somewhat English in manner, and carried a swagger stick. Ernest listened and watched with his customary care. . . . Miss Jessup might some day serve as a character in one of his stories.

Hemingway makes effective use of the little stick as a focusing point in the first meeting of Frederick Henry and Catherine Barkley in *A Farewell to Arms*:

> "How do you do?" Miss Barkley said. "You're not an Italian, are you?"

"Oh, no."

Rinaldi was talking to the other nurse. They were laughing.

"What an odd thing—to be in the Italian army."

"It's not really the army. It's only the ambulance."

"It's very odd though. Why did you do it?"

"I don't know," I said. "There isn't always an explanation for everything."

"Oh, isn't there? I was brought up to think there was."

"That's awfully nice."

"*Do* we have to go on and talk this way?"

"No," I said.

"That's a relief. Isn't it?"

"What's the stick?" I asked. Miss Barkley was quite tall. She wore what seemed to me to be a nurse's uniform, was blonde and had a tawny skin and gray eyes. I thought she was very beautiful. She was carrying a thin rattan stick like a toy riding crop, bound in leather.

"It belonged to a boy who was killed last year."

"I'm awfully sorry."

"He was a very nice boy. He was going to marry me and he was killed in the Somme."

"It was a ghastly show."

"Were you there?"

"No."

"I've heard about it," she said. "There's not really any war of that sort down here. They sent me the little stick. His mother sent it to me. They returned it with his things."

"Had you been engaged long?"

"Eight years. We grew up together."

"And why didn't you marry?"

"I don't know," she said. "I was a fool not to. I should have given him that anyway. But I thought it would be bad for him."

"I see."

"Have you ever loved anyone?"

"No," I said.

We sat down on a bench and I looked at her.

"You have beautiful hair," I said.

"Do you like it?"

"Very much."

"I was going to cut it off when he died."

"No."

"I wanted to do something for him. You see I didn't care about the other thing and he could have had it all. He could have had anything he wanted if I would have known. I would have married him or anything. I know all about it now. But then he wanted to go to war and I didn't know."

I did not say anything.

"I didn't know about anything then. I thought it would be worse for him. I thought perhaps he couldn't stand it and then of course he was killed and that was the end of it."

The effort here is to move the conversation of these two people on, from first meeting each other to the important isues that will carry the novel forward. Catherine tells Frederick that the little stick belonged to a boy who was killed in the war, and the conversation turns to the dead boy. Frederick changes the subject to Catherine's beautiful hair, but she relates that also to her dead lover, and continues almost hysterically to say she would have given him anything if she had only known what she knows now. So the author has brought the scene, in a few short lines, to the main thread of the novel, and to a foreshadowing of its development, like the warning tolling of a bell.

Variety in Dialogue

Long pages of dialogue can become as monotonous and skippable as any other methods of storytelling. The telling implication, the meaningful gesture, both can be included for variation. Dialogue should be short and to the point, but the accompanying stage directions enlarge upon meanings and implications.

Also useful is varying camera distance, moving closer in slowed time or back in speeded up time.

In the following scene from my novel *The Adelita*, the setting is the Mexican Revolution, the year 1916, when the United States was beginning to worry about preparation for World War I. Robert MacBean has served with the Mexican revolutionary army. His father, who has worried about his safety, has found him in Veracruz. The dialogue varies from summary to indirect discourse to direct, to thoughts, speculations by MacBean as to his father's mental processes, and includes gesture, facial expression and action, in order to move the passage swiftly and effectively:

I asked what "preparedness" meant.

"It means our being ready to fight the hun," my father said in a voice shaky with emotion. It was ignominy that we had not yet entered the war to aid our friends the French, Belgians and English against the hun; he, who had never been to a war, was contemptuous of President Wilson, who had kept America out of it.

"If I was your age—" he started. He was then fifty-two, I calculated. "It is the greatest war in the history of mankind," he said.

I said I had had enough of war to last at least that long, thank you. He stared at me with his jaw bunched. I had a disturbing sense of having become something to him that I had never been before.

"Of course you'd feel that way!" he said, fiercely, fondly. "They killed poor Frank, did they?"

I nodded and squeezed lime into my beer.

"And you were with Obregon's fellows. Sonorans."

"With Obregon." I listened to what he was resisting saying to me: *I knew you should never I was crazy with worry when you Couldn't you have Why didn't*

"Well, you are safe now, Bobby. And you quit them."

I felt my lips stretching into the shape of a grin.

"They are a hellish bunch," he said, raising his whiskey glass. I didn't know whether he meant Obregon's fellows, or all Mexicans.

"Well, I was one of them," I said.

"I just meant they are not like us, Bobby." I saw him frown with embarrassment to remember that I was half Mexican. "You know what I mean," he said. "Hard for people like us to understand why they act the way they do, like animals sometimes. The huns the same."

"I understood well enough," I said.

The band was playing "Dixie" now, and he turned to watch them, in profile to me. He wore an expression of self-conscious severity, as though ignoring bad manners.

Later we walked along the quays. . . .

Here follow the novelist Elizabeth Bowen's Rules of Dialogue:
1. Dialogue should be brief.
2. It should add to the reader's present knowledge.
3. It should eliminate the routine exchanges of ordinary conversation.
4. It should convey a sense of spontaneity but eliminate the repetitiveness of real talk.
5. It should keep the story moving forward.
6. It should be revelatory to the speaker's character, both directly and indirectly.
7. It should show the relationships between people.

CHAPTER 6

Authority/ Point of View

He and his neighbors are watching the same show, but one seeing more where another sees less, one seeing black where the other sees white, one seeing big where the other sees small, one seeing coarse where the other sees fine. . . .

—HENRY JAMES, *THE ART OF THE NOVEL*

The contemporary writer's devices for contriving to help the reader become lost in the fiction, and to be unaware of the manipulation by the author, are: the dramatization of the work through the use of specifics and sensory impressions, the use of dialogue, and the establishment of a central authority *within* the work rather than outside of it.

Central authority was a problem that did not exist for Thackeray. He was it. He told his story as though relating it to children at bedtime. As *I*, he entered into the story with an Olympian arrogance and self-righteousness, and if readers were jerked out of the proscenium arch of the world of the novel by these authorial forays, too bad for them.

Since Henry James, the author has usually withdrawn offstage (paring his fingernails, as James Joyce put it) to be replaced by a point of view within the work. Authors no longer have the almighty authority that Thackeray possessed, and the awareness of their presence at the controls jiggers the reader out of absorption in the fiction.

Here is the opening paragraph of Anne Lamott's novel *Crooked Little Heart*:

Rosie and her friends were blossoming like spring, budding, lithe, agile as cats. They wore tiny dresses and skirts so short that their frilly satin tennis bloomers showed. Into their bloomers they tucked an extra tennis ball to extract when it was needed, as with sleight of hand, like pulling a rabbit out of a hat, a quarter from behind an ear. Their days were spent honing their games in lessons and practice, playing in tournaments, and, in between matches, watching each other compete, killing time, hanging out, playing Ping-Pong and endless games of cards. They were brown as berries, with feet as white as the moon; the sock lines at their ankles were as sharply drawn as saddle shoes. Rosie and her partner Simone Duvall were good, ranked number one in the girls fourteen-and-under in northern California. Cocky and devoted, they loved to be watched by almost everyone but their parents, loved to be watched by other kids, by their pros, by the other kids' pros, and by members of the clubs at which they played—the weekend duffers who'd look at Rosie Ferguson, thirteen years old and seventy wiry pounds, hitting the ball as hard as almost any man they knew, thick black curls whipping, Siamese blue eyes steely, impassive, twenty bullets in a row, over the net and in, frowning almost imperceptibly if she missed.

Who is showing us this, giving us this information? The author, Lamott as Thackeray. Almost at the end of the paragraph, the author makes a feeble effort at showing us these hotshot girl tennis players through the eyes of the old duffers at the clubs, but does not pursue it. This description is very fine; the similes excellent (excepting brown as berries): the sock line as sharply drawn as saddle shoes, the steely Siamese (cat) blue eyes.

Still, no one is watching, no one with an attitude. My contention is that this description lacks the more drama it might have had if it were given us through the eyes and consciousness of (1) a lesser player who envies Rosie Ferguson, (2) a better player who is threatened by her progress, (3) a mother whose own tennis career failed for some reason, (4) a father who loves his daughter past all reason, (5) the tennis pro whose own beloved daughter has a crippled leg, (6) a pedophile stalker, (7) an old club duffer remembering his own youth and cockiness, (8) etcetera. These fine descriptive details and the similes employed would be that much more potent (it seems to me) if at the same time, they were characterizing a spectator.

Consider the following:

"How have you been?"
  "Fine. And you?"

"How have you been?" Jack said.
  "Fine. And you?" Howard said.

"How," Jack said, "have you been?"
  And Howard replied at once, "Fine. And you?"

"How have you been?" Jack inquired anxiously.
  "Fine. And you?" Howard giggled.

Jack said: "How have you been?"
  "Fine," Howard replied, dully.
  Then, with a fierce smile, he added: "And you?"

In the last four passages above there is authorial intrusion, that is, the author himself or the authority character adding commentary on how the words of the two speakers are spoken and how they are to be interpreted emotionally.

Here is another example of authorial intrusion, from *Mystery Ride* by Robert Boswell. The point of view has been established with Quin:

"It's never too late," Quin insisted, his *melodious voice* soft and beseeching. Angela was unmoved, he could see, so he spoke to the young couple. "May I hold the baby?" he asked, and accepted the child from the girl. "You mustn't give up hope," he said. "Even when you're at the ebb of your resources, even if someone you love has let you down, you shouldn't despair. Your life may turn around in no time; the person you love may yet prove to be worthy of your embrace. It's never too late— that's my motto."

"Mine, too," the boy said. "It's never too late. That's what I've been saying, more or less. We just got to get settled, get our nose in the door, you know, and then it'll be okay."

"Exactly," Quin said, lifting the baby over his head. The *smiling child drooled into Quin's perfect pompadour*, and he lowered the baby. (Emphasis added.)

It is clear that Quin is a self-important klutz, but hard to believe he thinks of his own voice as melodious or his pompadour as perfect; nor can he see the child smiling and drooling into it. These are authorial intrusions, and they jerk the reader out of his absorption in the story. To my mind, this is carelessness on the part of the author.

Here is a passage from Ron Hansen's novel *Atticus*:

> . . . Atticus replaced the green tarpaulin that had sagged off the gas tank of his old Indian motorcycle. Then he looked out at the night and a high plains landscape that was being gently simplified by snow. His windburnt face was a cinnamon red, ice was on his gray moustache like candle wax, his fair blue eyes watered with cold. . . .

Here the author shifts from behind Atticus's eyes, where we see what he looks out at ("a high plains landscape . . . simplified by snow"), to then include his description in the picture. This works smoothly and seamlessly.

This is Lena Grove from Faulkner's *Light in August*:

> After she got to be a big girl she would ask her father to stop the wagon at the edge of town and she would get down and walk. She would not tell her father why she wanted to walk in instead of riding. He thought that it was because of the smooth streets, the sidewalks. But it was because she believed that the people who saw her and whom she passed on foot would believe that she lived in town too.

The apparent shift of point of view in the third sentence above does not seem to me an authorial slip. Lena Grove could easily know what her father thought, by means of conversations the author did not need to record.

Certainly the reader wants to believe the fiction before him. He will provide willing *suspension of disbelief*, but he expects the author to provide a climate of believability.

The author's decision as to how the point of view, the central authority, the *consciousness* of the fiction, is to be handled can be paralyzingly difficult, or so easy as to be automatic. Frederick Henry in *A Farewell to Arms,* Nick Carraway in *The Great Gatsby* and Huck Finn as first-person point of view narrators are automatically central intelligences. Mrs. Dalloway, Yossarian in *Catch-22* and Tom Sawyer are third-person point of view intelligences. Novels such as Faulkner's *The Sound and the Fury* and Don DeLillo's *Underworld* have shifting points of view, with the author's hand slightly revealed as the selector of those points of view.

An ancient device in the art of literature is to pretend a source of the story is other than the author whose name is attached: *Robinson Crusoe* pretends to be the actual narrative of a castaway; in *The Rime of the Ancient Mariner*, the wedding guest is detained to hear the terrible story with the reader as eavesdropper.

This is from Paul Auster's *City of Glass*:

> . . . Cervantes, if you remember, goes to great lengths to convince the reader that he is not the author. The book, he says, was written in Arabic by Cid Hamete Benengeli. Cervantes describes how he discovered the manuscript by chance one day in the market in Toledo. He hires someone to translate it for him into Spanish, and thereafter he presents himself as no more than the editor of the translation. In fact, he cannot even vouch for the accuracy of the translation itself.

No doubt with tongue in cheek, Gabriel García Márquez claims a similar Arab to be the true author of his *One Hundred Years of Solitude*.

Charlotte Brontë published *Jane Eyre* as an autobiography, with Currer Bell (her pseudonym) as editor.

In my novel *Warlock*, I employed a series of (fictional) journals of a storekeeper in the western town of the title. These were given the appearance of reality by their diction, and some readers took them as genuine, so much so that the Blaisedell family genealogist (Clay Blaisedell was a major character in the novel) wrote me to ask about this particular Blaisedell, who did not appear in the family genealogies.

In *The Adventures of Huckleberry Finn*, Huck as narrator congratulates Mr. Twain on the general truthfulness of *The Adventures of Tom Sawyer*, and in the process establishes his own authority within the novel that bears his name. His narrative voice establishes an authority the reader will follow to the end. The contrast of the voice of Huck in *The Adventures of Huckleberry Finn* to the authorial voice in *The Adventures of Tom Sawyer* is significant. *The Adventures of Huckleberry Finn* is an American classic, while Twain's authorial voice in *The Adventures of Tom Sawyer* is condescending, patronizing, dated, sentimental and, to the post–*Huckleberry Finn* consciousness, shocking:

> . . . he saw a new girl in the garden—a lovely little blue-eyed creature with yellow hair plaited into two long tails, white summer frock, and embroidered pantalettes. The fresh-crowned hero fell without firing a shot. A certain Amy Lawrence vanished out of his heart and left not even a memory of herself behind. . . .

My novel *The Children of the Sun* is set in sixteenth-century Mexico and is concerned with the Cabeza de Vaca journey, the first crossing of the North American continent by Europeans. Cabeza de Vaca was accompanied by three companions, and my problem was to choose which one was to be the central authority. Cabeza de Vaca described his fellows as a reasonable man (Dorantes), a fearful man (Castillo) and a sensual man (the Moorish slave Esteban). Cabeza de Vaca himself was God infested and slightly crazed. I chose Dorantes, the reasonable man, as the central consciousness, and third person rather than first since I thought trying to establish an authentic sixteenth-century Spanish voice would lie beyond my powers.

There is a great deal of technical gobbledygook connected with point of view. The *I* of first-person point of view is called the narrator, and there are reliable, unreliable and multiple narrators, as well as letter and journal narration. Third-person point of view can be close, distant, detached or multiple. Authority can also be omniscient or authorial; the omniscient author still turns up in blockbuster fiction. Latin American writers, in particular, sometimes use second person, the *you* form.

This is from the preamble to Wilkie Collins's *The Woman in White,* an 1860 English mystery novel:

> No circumstance of importance, from the beginning to the end of the disclosure, shall be related on hearsay evidence. When the writer of these introductory lines (Walter Hartright by name) happens to be more closely connected than others with the incidents to be recorded, he will be the narrator. When not, he will retire from the position of narrator; and his task will be continued, from the point at which he has left off, by other persons who can speak to the circumstances under notice from their own knowledge, just as clearly and positively as he has spoken before them.
>
> Thus, the story here presented will be told by more than one pen, as the story of an offence against the laws is told in court by more than one witness—with the same object, in both cases, to present the truth always in its most direct and intelligible aspect; and to trace the course of one complete series of events by making the persons who have been most closely connected with them, at each successive stage, relate their own experience, word for word.

This is a clear-cut rationale for the use of a revolving or serial team of narrators or point-of-view characters.

Here is a hypothetical problem in point of view, concerning a fictional dysfunctional family in San Jose, California. Father George and mother Janet of ten-year-old Jassy are divorced. George has remarried Ellie, who has two children, twelve-year-old John and fifteen-year-old Bonny. Jassy's brother is sixteen-year-old Ben. The divorce court judge has arranged that Jassy and Ben spend every other two weeks with their father, every other two weeks with their mother. However, Jassy is unhappy within her father's new family, and calls her mother in hysterics in the middle of the night to come and get her. This has put George, Janet and Jassy into therapy sessions with a child psychologist, Mrs. Lester. Is Jassy being molested? By her stepbrother, John, or stepsister, Bonny, her father, whom?

How is this story to be told, the core of mystery solved and Jassy brought to some kind of stasis? Who is the point of view? Her mother, her father, Mrs. Lester? What about Jassy herself? Young people's voices can be very beguiling. Jassy may not know exactly what is happening to her, or she may be trying to protect her father or her father's new family members. How about Bonny, who knows something is going on but is protective of her brother, her mother, her stepfather, or, contrarily, is too quick to assign blame? What about Ben, a calm voice, who loves his sister but knows she is a hysteric? What about Mrs. Lester, the trained, seen-it-all psychologist who is half-right in her assumptions, or completely wrong. All of these people can be treated in first person with their distinctive voices, or more distantly in third person. Is there someone superior to the situation, the judge in the divorce court, say, who is responsible for the custody arrangement and can take a more rational view of these troubled, self-protective and prejudiced people? What would be the most dramatically effective consciousness for observing this situation?

One method might include an outer authority from Mrs. Lester's half-right and limited point of view, with an inner voice of Jassy (from Mrs. Lester's notes and recall?), between the lines of which the reader can satisfyingly put together his own truth of the events as they differ from Mrs. Lester's. Another possibility would be a rotating system of points of view, as per Wilkie Collins above, everyone with his or her own rationalization for his or her actions or the lack of them, with the viewpoint character's own interest primary and Jassy's subordinate.

Each of the participants in the situation, like the characters of the Japanese film *Rashomon*, has a different slant on what has happened or is happening, and that slant becomes an influential component of the story that results from the use of that person's point of view.

Point of view can be subordinate to what the author feels the story should do, or, on the other hand, a powerful factor in determining how the story will resolve itself.

Balzac is certainly the all-time champ of the description of interiors. Here are two from his novel *Cousin Bette*. In each case the description is given through the eyes of a character to whom the contents of the room are very meaningful, and whose description is dramatized by a personality, situation and attitude:

> . . . the National Guardsman was examining the furnishings of the room in which he found himself. As he remarked the silk curtains, once red, but now faded to violet by the sun and frayed along the folds by long use, a carpet from which the colours had disappeared, chairs with the gilding rubbed off and their silk spotted with stains and worn threadbare in patches, his contemptuous expression was followed by satisfaction, and then by hope, in naive succession on his successful-shopkeeper's commonplace face. He was surveying himself in a glass above an old Empire clock, taking stock of himself, when the rustle of the Baroness's silk dress warned him of her approach. He at once struck an attitude.

Crevel, the guardsman, is a rich former perfumer who is in a bidding war with the baron of this establishment for the favors of a teenage courtesan. He is pleased by the shabbiness of the room, which shows him that the baron has ruined himself in their competition. He also has designs upon the baroness, and the evidence of financial embarrassment encourages him to make her an offer of providing the dowry for her young daughter, who cannot make a good marriage without it, in return for the baroness's sexual surrender and the baron's consequent humiliation.

The baron is in competition with the very rich Duke d'Herouville for the favors of the nymphet Josepha, and the richness and beauty of the duke's drawing-room shows him that he is out of luck. The description of the place is again dramatized by the emotions of the character experiencing them:

> . . . the Baron . . . stood dazzled, dumbfounded, in this drawing-room, whose three windows opened upon a fairytale garden, one of those gardens brought into existence in a month with soil carried to the site and flowers planted out almost in bloom, whose lawns seemed to have been produced by alchemists'

magic. It was not only the studied elegance that he found admirable—the gilding, the costly carving in the style known as Pompadour, the sumptuous materials—for any tradesman might have ordered and obtained these by the mere expenditure of an ocean of gold. . . .

Coming into the room as the baron hopelessly surveys his surroundings, Josepha says, "Ah! You understand now, old boy?"

First-Person Point of View

First-person narration has the immediate advantage of a strong and very personal voice, a vividness, an automatic authority, a speedy immersion in point of view and consequent trust of it.

See the easy flow of this passage from *Treasure Island*, the first sight of the old buccaneer coming to the Admiral Benbow Inn, observed by Jim Hawkins:

> I remember him as if it were yesterday, as he came plodding to the inn door, his sea-chest following behind him in a handbarrow, a tall, strong, heavy, nut-brown man; his tarry pigtail falling over the shoulders of his soiled blue coat; his hands ragged and scarred, with black, broken nails; and the sabre cut across one cheek, a dirty, livid white. I remember him looking round the cove and whistling to himself as he did so, and then breaking out in that old sea-song that he sang so often afterwards:
> "Fifteen men on the dead man's chest—
> Yo-ho-ho, and a bottle of rum."
> in the high, old tottering voice that seemed to have been tuned and broken at the capstan bars. Then he rapped on the door with a bit of stick like a handspike that he carried, and when my father appeared, called roughly for a glass of rum. This, when it was brought to him, he drank slowly like a connoisseur, lingering on the taste, and still looking about him at the cliffs and up at our signboard.

The old sea dog is closely observed, with three excellent details: his tarry pigtail, his ragged hands with their black and broken nails, and the sabre cut on his cheek. The verbs keep the description in motion, the sense perceptions are of sight and sound, the description and action specific and dramatic. The reader is very comfortable with Jim's first-person narration.

But there are a number of first-person caveats.

Henry James called first-person singular "that accurst autobiographic form which puts a premium on the loose, the improvised, the cheap and the easy." This rant may be unfair, but it is true that the author is apt to fall in love with his vivid voice and forget to rein it in, become overly garrulous, find accommodation for an excess of words just because they sound good and also use the narrative voice to cover inadequacies of plot and character.

The advice of the great Scribners editor Maxwell Perkins to F. Scott Fitzgerald on his first novel, *This Side of Paradise*, was that he rewrite the novel in third-person point of view rather than first-person narration, in order to gain more distance from his material. In other words, if the author and his character are to some degree similar, the iron clutch of actual events becomes a constraint to creatively changing what actually happened to what *should* happen fictionally.

A novice writer is apt to think that first-person narration gives fiction more immediacy. Not so. The essence of such an authority is that it is retrospective. These events have already occurred; they are being related by the narrator after the action has been completed.

It can be said that first-person fiction is written *backward*, from the end, while third person is written *forward*, from the beginning. Although both are equally written in the past tense, in the third-person authority there is the illusion of the action taking place before the reader's eyes. In first person the action has already taken place; thus, we know that the narrator has lived to tell the tale. When he hangs by a frayed rope over the pit of cobras, we know that he will not perish, for he is telling us what happened to him back then.

H.P. Lovecraft does not convince us of the death of I with these words:

> I hear footsteps on the stairs; they're coming for me: and God
> have mercy on my soul!

Nor does the ending of James M. Cain's *The Butterfly*:

> Here comes Blue. He's got a gun. He . . .

A popular contemporary form is the first-person present tense, with which the writer hopes to give the illusion that the events are happening to the *I* before the reader's eyes. It is much employed in contemporary short stories and carries a taint of the voguish.

Here is a passage from Jane Mendelsohn's *I Was Amelia Earhart*:

> In the middle of the night I go to the Electra for one of my midnight voyages. But by the time I get there, I've woken up completely, I'm no longer in a trance. I'm awake and I walk into the navigator's cabin. In my bare feet I walk on our charts, our maps, scraps of paper covered with calculations. . . .

The reader may decide whether this has more immediacy than "In the middle of the night I went to the Electra. . . ."

There are barriers that the first-person narrator cannot, except by means of artificial devices, get around. He can't reasonably present his own character or analyze his unconscious reactions and prejudices convincingly. In an action plot this may not be the drawback, but it is a handicap in a plot of character. There are difficulties of knowing what subsidiary characters are feeling, or what is going on outside the actual purview of the narrator. These gaps can only be filled in by the reports of others, a device that hinders the presentation of immediacy.

It is difficult for the author to describe the narrator without the use of some form of mirror or photograph, or in fact a trick.

Because the narrator's mind is presumably open to us, it is difficult to make believable the concealing of information from the reader. It is impossible, for instance, to keep the secret that the narrator is actually the Bay City Strangler.

On the other hand some of these limitations may be cleverly used to great advantage. The character does not know what is going on, but the reader can put clues together to realize more than the character does. There can be considerable suspense gained by this. Will Joan realize before her policeman lover goes out the door that the stove repairman conducting his work in the kitchen is not what he seems to be?

The following dialogue between Else and her husband, John, is from the chilling story "The Yellow Wallpaper" by Charlotte Perkins Gilman:

> I thought it was a good time to talk, so I told him that I really was not gaining here, and that I wished he would take me away.
>
> "Why, darling," said he, "our lease will be up in three weeks and I can't see how to leave before.
>
> "The repairs are not done at home, and I cannot possibly leave town just now. Of course if you were in any danger, I could and would, but you really are better, dear, whether you can see it or not. I am a doctor, dear, and I know. You are gaining flesh and color, your appetite is better, I feel really much easier about you."
>
> "I don't weigh a bit more," said I, "nor as much; and my appetite may be better in the evening when you are here, but it is worse in the morning when you are away!
>
> "Bless her little heart!" said he with a big hug, "she shall be as sick as she pleases! But now let's improve the shining hours by going tosleep, and talk about it in the morning!"
>
> "And you won't go away?" I asked gloomity. "Why, how can I, dear? It is only three weeks more and then we will have a nice little trip of a few days while Jennie is getting the house ready. Really dear you are better!"
>
> "Better in body perhaps—" I began, and stopped short, for he sat up straight and looked at me with such a stern, reproach-ful look that I could not say another word.
>
> "My darling," said he, "I beg of you, for my sake and for our child's sake, as well as for your own, that you will never for one instant let that idea enter your mind! There is nothing so dangerous, so fascinating, to a temperament like yours. It is a false and foolish fancy. Can you not trust me as a physician when I tell you so?"
>
> So of course I said no more on that score. . . .

The reader knows better than to trust anyone who says *dear* and *darling* so much as John, and talks about his wife to her in the third person. Else is in terrible danger and the reader knows it, but Else does not.

In the contemporary American classic *One Flew Over the Cuckoo's Nest*, the story is a stock one, as the author Ken Kesey points out. What makes the novel so remarkable is the narrative voice, the crazed, ultraperceptive vison of the paranoid-schizophrenic Chief Broom:

> They're out there.
>
> Black boys in white suits up before me to commit sex acts in the hall and get it mopped up before I can catch them.
>
> They're mopping when I come out of the dorm, all three of them sulky and hating everything, the time of day, the place they're at here, the people they got to work around. When they hate like this, better if they don't see me. I creep along the wall quiet as dust in my canvas shoes, but they got special sensitive equipment detects my fear and they all look up, all three at once, eyes glittering out of the black faces like the hard glitter of radio tubes out of the back of an old radio.
>
> "Here's the Chief. The soo-pah Chief, fellas. Ol' Chief Broom. . . ."

Here is a narrator, from my *The Coming of the Kid*:

> My name is Frank Pearl, and first off I will say something about myself. I am a man that knows being small has disadvantages, that's for certain. Looking another man always in the placket instead of the eye does not give the best impression of human nature, but a small fellow will sometimes notice things that might be beneath a regular-size person. For instance, once when I was making water and eating an apple at the same time, I noticed that the odor of piddle made the smell of that apple stand out, a fine smell that I'd never noticed before. Now a fellow whose nose is further away from his private parts might not have noticed that. Since then I have made experiments with many other varieties of fruit, and I have discovered that it is

the peach that smells the most satisfying in this context. I am a born experimenter, with an interest in all natural phenomena (and unnatural too), especially in herbs and medicines. Famous for it in the Territory.

For instance, it was my gunshot salve that saved the Kid's life the time he was shot.

This paragraph goes a long way toward characterizing Frank Pearl in his role as a healer, establishing his dwarfness and the historical pastness of the piece through colloquialisms such as "that's for certain" and "Famous for it in the Territory." The reader will trust the words of this narrator.

Read this first paragraph of Charles Portis's *True Grit*:

People do not give it credence that a 14-year-old girl could leave home and go off in the wintertime to avenge her father's blood, but it did not seem so strange then, although I will say that it did not happen every day. I was just 14 years of age when a coward going by the name of Tom Cheney shot my father down in Fort Smith, Arkansas, and robbed him of his life and his horse and $150 in cash money plus two California gold pieces, which he carried in his trouser band.

That's a voice and a narrator also to trust and treasure. As is Joan Didion's heroine's peculiar narrative voice in *Play It As It Lays*:

What makes Iago evil, some people ask. I never ask. Another example which springs to mind because Mrs. Burstein saw a pygmy rattler in the artichoke garden this morning and has been intractable since: I never ask about snakes. Why should a coral snake need two glands of neurotoxic poison to survive while a king snake so similarly marked needs none? Where is the Darwinian logic there. You might ask that. I never would, not any more.

Didion presents us with a character of terrific interest, and also causes us to be anxious to know what has happened as this story moves from its ending (now) back to its beginning, to make her this way.

Here is the beginning of Alice Walker's novel *The Color Purple,* Celie's first letter to God:

> Dear God,
>
> My mama dead. She die screaming and cussing. She scream at me. She cuss at me. I'm big. I can't move fast enough. By time I git back from the well, the water be warm. By the time I git the tray ready the food be cold. By time I git the children ready for school it be dinner time. He don't say nothing. He set there by the bed holding her hand an cryin, talking bout don't leave me, don't go.
>
> She ast me bout the first one Whose it is? I say God's. I don't know no other man or what else to say. When I start to hurt and then my stomach start moving and then that little baby come out my pussy chewing on it fist you could have knock me down with a feather.
>
> Don't nobody come see us.
>
> She got sicker an sicker.
>
> Finally she ast Where it is?
>
> I say God took it.
>
> He took it. He took it while I was sleeping. Kilt it out there in the woods. Kill this one too, if he can.

This passage seems as simple as the confused young girl who enunciates it, but it is full of craft. Three people are introduced, a plot is set in motion and a line of horror is kindled in Celie's bare language of stunning authenticity.

When the writer is dealing with a larger-than-life character, say Sherlock Holmes, Willie Stark in *All the King's Men* or Jay Gatsby of *The Great Gatsby*, the first-person narrator probably should not be that character himself; better to employ a subsidary character as narrator, a Doctor Watson, Jack Burden or Nick Carraway, a man of thought regarding a man of action.

Similarly, a child who imperfectly understands what and who is going on around him presents a very effective authority; Maisie in Henry James's *What Maisie Knew*, Mattie of *True Grit* observing Rooster Cogburn, or

Jim Hawkins in *Treasure Island* with an imperfect understanding of Long John Silver.

The "innocent eye" is a staple of American fiction. Shane observed by a hero-worshipping boy is more effective than Shane as a third-person point-of-view protagonist.

The most immediate means of expressing character in the point-of-view character or narrator of the novel is through the verisimilitude of the sensory perceptions and in the authority of the language in which these are expressed.

First-Person Narration:

> I jammed the lawnmower in a series of slashes around the trunk of the Chinese elm, and cast a hawk eye up at Miranda's bedroom window where the shade hung half closed like a wink. A fifteen-year-old girl didn't have any right to be out half the night with a pimple-faced high school punk. I'd turned on the night light when I'd heard them shuffling on the front porch: 2:19!
>
> I took a look at myself in the shiny chrome hubcap that had fallen from a passing car, rolled into the yard and finished its flight leaning against the bole of the pepper tree. I saw a swollen, distorted reflection of a disapproving father; tall, skinny, black-headed with hair starting to thin on top, shine of sweat on his forehead. . . .

Here is the first-person advantage of an immediately engaging and character-establishing voice. However, as the author is divorced from the narrative, information he might have offered economically can only be supplied with a great deal of circumlocution, for instance, the maneuver resorted to above to bring the reader a description of the *I*, who cannot even be named without the employment of some device.

Third-Person Point of View

John Fowles has said: "The great majority of modern third-person narration is 'I' narration thinly disguised."

Except for pronouns, the difference can be slight, although there is at some level a consciousness that third person is taking place before the reader's eyes, while first person is being related (and dramatized) after the fact. The voice is less of a factor in third person, with consequent less intensity, but on the other side of the ledger there can be greater flexibility and variety. The camera can be manipulated, to rest behind the viewpoint character's eyes, or to rise and back up to include him in its frame.

Here's an example showing third-person point of view treating the same scene and material as above.

Third-Person Narration:

> David Brady pushed the lawnmower in a series of slashes around the trunk of the Chinese elm. Sweat stung in his eyes and felt slick like syrup on his hands. He was tall and dark-skinned, with a bald spot beginning in the midst of his unruly black hair and a triangular scar on his cheekbone that made him look as though he had a headache. There was a churn in his chest midway between anxiety and anger as he halted to mop at his forehead with his bandanna, glancing up at the second-story window where his daughter's shade hung at half-mast. Miranda had gone out with a pimple-faced, testosterone-loaded high school jerk last night and hadn't come home until two in the morning.

Here we begin in a fairly close third-person point of view, with sense impressions felt by David (sweat stinging in his eyes and feeling slick on his hands), but then the author sneaks in to describe David for the reader, and to inform her of his feelings about his daughter's evening. So this passage moves rather effortlessly from close third person to more distant, including David in the camera's eye with a summary of David's appearance and mental state presented in a much more economical form than could have been managed in the earlier narration.

This passage could move even farther away from David's point of view without shaking the reader's credulity:

He was not yet aware of his daughter's excuse, which was a flat tire suffered with no spare. The fact that the tire had been punctured at the local and infamous Neckers' Paradise was not information that would be proffered to him.

Here is James Joyce, from his short story "The Dead":

Gabriel had not gone to the door with the others. He was in a dark part of the hall gazing up the staircase. A woman was standing near the top of the first flight, in the shadow also. He could not see her face but he could see the terracotta and salmon-pink panels of her skirt, which the shadow made appear black and white. It was his wife. She was leaning on the bannister, listening to something. . . .

This is almost cinematographic, where the camera reveals the observing character then switches to show what the character sees.

Here is the opening of the novel *Charlotte Gray* by Sebastian Faulks:

Peter Gregory kicked the door of the dispersal hut closed behind him with the heel of his boot. He sensed the iciness of the air outside but was too well wrapped to feel it on his skin. He looked up and saw a big moon hanging still, while ragged clouds flew past and broke up like smoke in the darkness. He began to waddle across the grass, each step won from the limits of movement permitted by the parachute that hung down behind him as he bucked and tossed his way forward. He heard the clank of the corporal fitter's bicycle where it juddered over the ground to his right. . . .

This is an airman in his warm flight suit leaving the dispersal hut and crossing the tarmac toward his airplane, being joined along the way by the fitter, who is a corporal. Peter Gregory's point of view is established, and his senses invoked: the iciness of the air, the sight of the big moon and scudding clouds, the sound of the fitter's bicycle, the awkwardness of his parachute. The scene is in action, and the verbs are fixed in Peter's sense perceptions and physical sensations: *kicked, flew, broke up, waddle, bucked and tossed, juddered.*

A consistent point of view can produce a powerful unifying factor in a piece of fiction. Changing point of view, especially in short fiction, risks unravelling the authority that gives the work credence, although contemporary writers have become very clever at using point-of-view shifts to dramatic purpose.

In the scene of the fight between the brothers in Ken Kesey's *Sometimes a Great Notion*, the author manipulates point of view in a daring manner, employing lowercase, capitals and parentheses to present Lee's and Hank's. Viv, the cause of the fight, is watching the action:

> We reeled and shuffled from the dock up onto the gravelly bank; we rocked and rolled down the bank through a litter of roadside garbage. Always with Andy right beside us, cheering neither one nor the other of us. Always with Viv's voice trickling out of gray distance, pleading with Hank to stop. Always with that other voice screaming from a much closer gray— IMBECILE—and demanding the same thing of me: STOP FIGHTING! RUN FOR YOUR LIFE! HE'LL KILL YOU!
>
> (Like everlastingly pestering a man who has a gun until the man—But why does he keep on?)
>
> YOU KNOW YOU CAN'T BEAT HIM. IF YOU KEEP FIGHTING HE'LL KILL YOU. LIE DOWN! STOP!
>
> (Like prodding a bear with a stick until—But if he knows that already why is he—?)
>
> HE'LL KILL YOU, Old Reliable kept screeching, LIE DOWN! But something had happened. In a fist fight there is a point, after a cheek has been split or a nose broken with a sound in your skull like a light bulb being popped in mud, when you realize that you have already survived the worst. DON'T GET BACK UP! the voice from the shadows insisted as I struggled to free myself from a deep green net of berry vines where I had been thrown by a booming, eye-closing right. JUST LIE HERE. IF YOU GET UP HE'LL KILL YOU!

And the voice, for the first time in a long, long reign over my psyche, met with opposition. "No," said a stranger in my head. "Not so."

YES, IT IS SO. LIE STILL. IF YOU GET UP HE'LL KILL YOU.

"Not so," the voice dissented again, calmly. "No, he can't kill you. He's already done his damndest. You've survived the worst."

The master point of view here is with the narrator, Lee, who is fighting his older brother, Hank, of whom he is terrified. The voice of his terror (Old Reliable) is in capitals; Hank's voice is in parentheses. There is a brief authorial voice discussing the sequences of a fistfight.

A talented young writer is having a grand time exploring the possibilities of switching points of view. The argument of points of view within Lee's head seems to me effective. Hank's voice, however, in parentheses, is less successful.

The issue of changing point of view can be a challenge to the authors of novels. Maintaining a single point of view may be limiting, while an overly casual shifting from consciousness to consciousness will reveal the author as manipulator and detract from the reality of the fiction. A common solution is changing by chapters, perhaps labeled with the name of the character serving as the authority within. Changing by paragraphs is a much riskier business.

A rule of thumb is that the gains of changing point of view ought to outweigh the losses.

In the following passage from *Madame Bovary*, it is interesting to observe the care with which Flaubert accomplishes a point-of-view shift. The point of view originates with Rodolphe, who has written a letter to Emma ending their adulterous relationship, and which is to be carried to Emma by the ploughboy Girard:

He re-read his letter. He considered it very good.

"Poor little woman!" he thought with emotion. "She'll think me harder than a rock. There ought to have been some tears on this; but I can't cry; it isn't my fault." Then, having emptied some water into a glass, Rodolphe dipped a finger into it, and he let a big drop fall on the paper, that made a pale stain on the ink. Then looking for a seal, he came upon the one *"Amor del cor."*

"That doesn't at all fit in with the circumstances. Pshaw! never mind!"

After which he smoked three pipes and went to bed.

The next day when he was up (at about two o'clock—he had slept late), Rodolphe had a basket of apricots picked. He put his letter at the bottom under some vine leaves, and at once ordered Girard, the ploughman, to take it with care to Madame Bovary. He made use of this means for corresponding with her, sending according to the season fruits or game.

"If she asks after me," he said, "you will tell her that I have gone on a journey. You must give the basket to her herself, into her own hands. Get along and take care!"

Girard put on his new blouse, knotted his handkerchief round the apricots, and walking with great heavy steps in his thick iron-bound galoshes, made his way to Yonville.

Madame Bovary, when he got to her house, was arranging a bundle of linen at the kitchen-table with Felicite.

"Here," said the ploughboy, "is something for you from the master."

She was seized with apprehension, and as she sought in her pocket for some coppers, she looked at the peasant with haggard eyes, while he himself looked at her with amazement, not understanding how such a present could move anyone. At last he went out. Felicite remained. She could bear it no longer; she ran into the sitting room as if to take the apricots there, overturned the basket, tore away the leaves, found the letter, opened it, and, as if some fearful fire were behind her, Emma flew to her room terrified.

Charles was there; she saw him; he spoke to her; she heard nothing, and she went on quickly up the stairs, breathless, distraught, dumb, and ever holding this horrible piece of paper, that crackled between her fingers like a plate of sheet iron.

From Rodolphe the letter accompanies the basket of fruit, and Girard with his great heavy steps, to be passed to Emma, between whose fingers it crackles like a plate of sheet iron. The point of view has been smoothly shifted.

Second-Person Point of View

Second-person point of view has a tour de force quality, as in Jay McInerney's *Bright Lights, Big City* or Fay Weldon's *Letters to Alice on First Reading Jane Austen*. It is often employed in Latin-American novels. Carlos Fuentes uses second person as one of several points of view of the same character in *Where the Air is Clear*, where the second person is that of an aging Mexican politico looking back at his actions, heroic, brutal or cowardly, during the Mexican Revolution. This point of view is used in a self-incriminating manner, and by its nature the usage tends to convey an accusatory tone.

The following is from Fuentes's *A Change of Skin*:

> Words were not for night when you lay together very simply in the plain white room with the white beams and the white chimney. And you could think with great clarity then, clearly and subtly because wrapped in each other's arms in the fisherman's bed you believed that together you were holding, forming, the parts of a very brief past.

In this novel there is an actual *you* narrator, whose identity is revealed only on the final page.

This is from Jay McInerney's *Bright Lights, Big City*:

> Your head is pounding with voices of confession and revelation. You follow the trails of white powder across the mirror in pursuit of a point of convergence where everything was cross-referenced according to a master code. For a second, you felt terrific. You were coming on grips. Then the coke ran out; as you hoovered the last line, you saw yourself hideously close-up with a rolled twenty sticking out of your nose. The goal is receding. Whatever it was. You can't get everything straight in

one night. You are too excited to think any more and too exhausted to sleep. If you lie down you are afraid you might die.

The point of view in here is actually first person, with the narrator speaking accusingly to himself as *you*.

Omniscient Point of View

Complete privilege is what we may call omniscient narration. Elements in the fiction that reveal the author as narrator and manipulator will distance the reader from it, but the omniscient narrator can tell us a good deal about those aspects of the tale that, though necessary, are not entitled to the heightening that would come if they were dramatized. The overall effect can be to make us feel that we have been given a better story, more carefully worked, than would have been possible if the author had simply served up his materials in a more restrictive format.

The great narrators always managed to find some way to make their narrations gripping, and there are times when we do surrender ourselves to such authors, some readers more readily than others.

Judith Krantz may not be another Fielding, but she knows how to make her narrations compelling. The author of *Princess Daisy* is an omniscient author of considerable powers.

This is from the first page of that novel. Daisy is introduced atop the Empire State Building in conversation with the official in charge of the Observation Deck. This man is of no consequence to the novel, but the author dips into his point of view to describe Daisy, knowing that information given by a character is more effective than that given by the author:

> The uniformed official looked up at Daisy with perplexed admiration and dismay. He didn't understand anything about her. She was young and more beautiful than anyone he'd ever seen but she wore a man's moldy baseball jacket which bore the now mournful legend BROOKLYN DODGERS on its back, a pair of United States Navy sailor pants, and dirty tennis shoes. He was far from a romantic man, but everything about her stung his imagination with an unaccustomed fascination. He found

himself curiously unable to look away from her. She was as tall as he, at least five feet, seven inches, and something about the way she walked had suggested the balance of the trained athlete even before she had jumped up to the perch from which she now gestured, intrepid, light-hearted, as if she were trying to catch a beam of the sun itself. The roof supervisor was aware of a particular clarity and cadence in her speech that made him think she wasn't American, yet who but an American would dress like that? When she'd first appeared all she'd asked was for permission to film a commercial on his roof and now she was hanging up there like a goddamned angel on a Christmas tree. . . .

At the end of the scene Judith Krantz retreats to her authorial authority and informs us of Daisy's actual status.

The dramatic method, by direct presentation (here the point of view of the roof supervisor), seeks to give the reader a sense of being present at the scene of the action. Those elements are undramatic that make the reader aware that it is the author who is explaining things, such as the revelation that Daisy is actually the Princess Marguerite Alexandrovna Valensky.

The most obvious task for the omniscient author is to tell the reader facts she could not easily learn otherwise. There are many kinds of facts, of course: explanations of the meaning of an action, summaries of thought processes, or of events too insignificant to merit being dramatized, description of physical events and details, whenever such description cannot spring naturally from a character. Revealing in dialogue or action the fact that Daisy is actually a princess, for instance, would be a lengthy and complicated process.

In the opening pages of *Breath and Shadows* by Ella Leffland, there is in authorial reporting a scene of two children racing downstairs with a captive cat. The author then enters the cat's consciousness to give his assessment of the children and especially of his mistress, whom he loves. Next we switch into the point of view of the maid, a simple and rather pushy country girl, who gives us a more comprehensive view of the house and its occupants, including something of the history of how she came here, and of how much she likes her employers, a generous, easygoing and comely young couple. Finally we are taken into the point of view of the couple themselves, assured of their worth and goodness by the opinions of cat and maid. All this is handled deftly, although with a low level of intensity and a certain unsureness on the part of the reader as to who is to be given particular attention and sympathy.

Information

The novel has always been intimately involved with information, indeed the title of the genre itself refers to "the new," the presentation of the what's new? of information to the evolving middle class.

Information presented directly by the author tends to become a lecture. It should be dramatized. The simplest means of dramatization is the use of an authority within the novel, that is, point of view.

Naturalistic novelists such as Zola employed a kind of expert witness formula for presenting information. A character would be produced solely for the purpose of conveying information to the reader. Henry James also used a character, whom he called a ficelle, as a partner in a dialogue with the protagonist that provided the reader with necessary information for plot and character development.

Here is an informational passage from Robert Stone's novel *Damascus Gate*:

> The other outfits, whose representatives had been in attendance at the radio shack, both Zimmer and the American rabbi regarded as potentially useful idiots.
>
> One of these groups, founded by another American, in this case the renegade Hasid, had its roots among the Essenes and the Books of Jubilees and Enoch. It made an effort to proselytize among the Ethiopian Jews, for whom those texts held great importance. Its aim was to restore the balance of time as conveyed to Moses by the angel Uriel, so that the feasts might be celebrated as the Almighty desired. . . .
>
> Another sect in attendance, represented at the meeting by

its founder, was the creation of Mike Glass, a junior-college professor of Jewish background who had grown up in an anti-Semitic New England town and lived a secular life. After teaching poly sci and coaching football, he had turned to Jewish studies following the breakup of his marriage.

He had come to the Apocalypse through his readings of Scripture, the agrarian pessimism of Wendell Berry and the predestinarian poetry of Larry Woiwode. The history of Israel, he felt, provided evidence of divine election and the human depravity from which only God's choice could rescue humankind.

Raziel Melker had also attended, representing, in a way, the disciples of Adam de Kuff. Neither de Kuff nor Sonia, nor anyone else close to them, knew about Raziel's association with Zimmer and his attendance at the meeting.

Stone is providing information on the multitudinous Christian, Jewish and Moslem sects that contend in Jerusalem. There is a feeble pretense that this information comes to us through Zimmer and the American rabbi, but in fact it is authorial. This is of course an efficient method, but the scene might have more dramatic force if presented through the intelligence of the protagonist, Lucas, who is a student of these sects and who plans to write a book about them—seemingly a conception exactly designed for disbursing this kind of information.

In *American Pastoral*, Philip Roth is a fountain of information on a number of subjects—prostate cancer, glovemaking, Miss America contests, the history of Newark, New Jersey, in the Revolutionary War, fine breeds of milk cattle and more. In the following scene the subject is glovemaking, the art and craft and industry that the protagonist's father has lovingly passed along to him. The Swede is presenting this information to the reader by means of a ficelle, Rita Cohen, whom Swede Levov is showing through his glove manufactory:

> From a wrapped-up bundle of hides dampening beside Harry, he picked one out in a pale shade of brown. "This is a tough color to get," the Swede told her. "British tan. You can see,

there's all sorts of variation in the color—see how light it is down here? Okay. This is sheepskin. What you saw in my office was pickled. This has been tanned. This is leather. But you can still see the animal. If you were to look at the animal," he said, "here it is—the head, the butt, the front legs, the hind legs, and here's the back, where the leather is harder and thicker, as it is over our own backbones . . ."

Honey. He began calling her honey up in the cutting room and he couldn't stop, and this even before he understood that by standing beside her he was as close to Merry as he had been since the general store blew up and his honey disappeared. This is a French ruler, it's about an inch longer than an American ruler. . . . This is called a spud knife, dull, beveled to an edge but not sharp. . . . Now he's pulling the trank down like that, to the length again—Harry likes to bet you that he'll pull it right down to the pattern without even touching the pattern, but I don't bet him because I don't like losing. . . . This is called a fourchette. . . . See, all meticulously done. . . . He's going to cut yours and give it to me so we can take it down to the making department. . . . This is called a slitter, honey. Only mechanical process in the whole thing. A press and a die, and the slitter will take about four tranks at a time. . . .

"Wow. This is an elaborate process," said Rita.

"That it is. Hard to really make money in the glove business because it is so labor-intensive—a time-consuming process, many operations to be coordinated. Most of the glove businesses have been family businesses. From father to son. Very traditional business. A product is a product to most manufacturers. The guy who makes them doesn't know anything about them. The glove business isn't like that. This business has a long long history."

"Do other people feel the romance of the glove business the way you do, Mr. Levov? You really are mad for this place and the processes. I guess that's what makes you a happy man."

"Am I?" he asked, and felt as though he were going to be

dissected, cut into by a knife, and all his misery revealed. "I guess I am."

The subtext here is that glovemaking is a family business, passed down to the Swede by his immigrant father, but American glovemaking is a doomed industry, for there are no more workers interested in the fine workmanship necessary, like the master cutter Harry. The Swede mentions the passing on from father to son of the craft. He loved and revered his father, as he loves America, and as he loves his daughter Merry. His radical-guerrilla daughter, however, hates him for a bourgeois and a capitalist and (this is the sixties) hates America also. She has planted a bomb in the post-office general store to bring the Vietnam War home, and killed a man. Merry is in hiding, and her father's life is ruined. The Swede, then, is presenting information to the reader by way of the ficelle, Rita, who is an emissary from and stand-in for his daughter, in a very highly charged context. This information has been dramatized.

✤ CHAPTER 7 ✤

Characterization

What is character but determination of incident? What is incident but the illustration of character?

—HENRY JAMES, *THE ART OF THE NOVEL*

C haracters are what the reader is interested in. It is through characters that he leads the extracurricular, imaginary and substitute life that is fiction's gift, and it is through the adventures, antics and predicaments of the characters that he may learn lessons that pertain to the conduct of his own life. The plot or story that is the result of the characters' will and antics (or vice versa) is of interest insofar as the characters are of interest. Therefore the first problem for the writer is the creation of characters.

Characters may not be created so much as *found*. Most often they are found in pieces, a trait here, a resemblance there, plus some happy invention. They reveal themselves slowly to the author; they come together not all at once but in the course of the actual writing.

Thomas Mann would have the writer observe in an obsessive manner:

> The look that one directs at things, both outward and inward,
> as an artist, is not the same as that with which one would regard
> the same as a man, but at once colder and more passionate. As
> a man, you might be well-disposed, patient, loving, positive,
> and have a wholly uncritical inclination to look upon everything
> as all right, but as an artist your daemon constrains you to
> "observe," to take note, lightning fast and with hurtful malice,

of every detail that in the literary sense would be characteristic, distinctive, significant, opening insights, typifying the race, the social or the psychological mode, recording all as mercilessly as though you had no human relationship to the observed object whatever.

Mann is interested in the clues a sociologist or a psychologist would look for in examining a patient, or Sherlock Holmes in taking the measure of a new client.

Sidney Sheldon, in his thriller *The Doomsday Conspiracy,* shows us the world leaders discussing Navy Commander Robert Bellamy, who has been assigned to investigate The Conspiracy. The italics are Sheldon's:

"Who are we using?" The Russian. *Huge. Short-tempered.*

"His name is Commander Robert Bellamy."

"How was he selected?" The German. *Aristocratic. Ruthless.*

"The Commander was chosen after a thorough computer search of the files of the CIA, FBI, and a half dozen other security agencies."

"Please, may I enquire what are his qualifications?" The Japanese. *Polite. Sly.*

The Englishman is *snobbish, dangerous;* the Frenchman *argumentative, stubborn*; the Chinese *clever, patient.* This is a lame effort to create the characters by the employment of abstractions, which are also racial and national clichés.

As F. Scott Fitzgerald said, "Begin with an individual and before you know it you have created a type; begin with a type, and you find that you have created—nothing."

As Elizabeth Bowen puts it in an essay on fiction, "The Mulberry Tree," "Characters must *materialize*—i.e., must have palpable physical reality. They must be not only see-able (vizualizable); they must be . . . felt."

An entity must be produced upon the page who breathes, walks across the room, leaves footprints in the snow, has fingerprints, odor, cavities, a hairdo, seeing eyes, hearing ears and all the other senses.

The Methods of Developing Character

1. Point of View
(See Chapter 6)

2. Exposition

Exposition violates the classical authorial imperative of "Show don't tell." When fiction "shows" it reaches what Conrad calls the "secret springs of responsive emotion." When fiction "tells" it is expository and informational, and does not "take." However, if *everything* in a fiction is shown, it becomes dense, circumlocutory, overly subtle and wasteful, while exposition can be dramatized by the use of specific detail and sensory perceptions.

Compromise is necessary. The following factual material has italicized sensory detail added:

> He roomed with a family named Jones on Pine Street, and made his ablutions at the Kearny Street Baths *with their steamy atmosphere and duckboards as soft as carpeting.* Hiram Jones was a carpenter who suffered from "the weakness" and did not work much, except to make repairs on his house and sit on the stoop observing street passages *and emanating whiskey fumes and belching at the clusters of prostitutes parading past in their finery.*
>
> Mrs. Jones was the harried keeper of a boardinghouse with four male boarders who shared dinners *always the lovely brown joint in the oven on Sundays filling the house with its anticipatory odors* with her and Mr. Jones and the young Joneses aged five to thirteen, the oldest being pretty Marjorie *in her frilly dresses and patent-leather shoes that gleamed like stars.*

As can be seen, a passage of pure exposition may be dramatized by the addition of sensory specifics so that there is a gain of economy while the exposition is raised out of the flatness of telling.

The details also reveal character in terms of their very choice, and the manner in which they are conveyed to the reader.

3. Description

In showing character, description can vary from the flattest of exposition to the subtlest of implication. Here is Uncle Ray, from Laurie Lee's *The Edge of Day*:

> I awoke one morning to find snoring beside me a huge and scaly man. I touched the thick legs and knotted arms and pondered the barbs on his chin, felt the crocodile flesh of this magnificent creature and wondered what it could be.
>
> "It's your Uncle Ray come home," whispered Mother. "Get up now and let him sleep."
>
> I saw a rust-brown face, a gaunt Indian nose, and smelt a reek of cigars and train oil. He was the hero of our school-boasting days, and to look on him was no disappointment. He was shiny as iron, worn as a rock, and lay like a chieftain sleeping. He'd come home on a visit from building his railway, loaded with money and thirst, and the days he spent in our house that time were full of wonder and conflagration.
>
> For one thing he was unlike any other man we'd ever seen— or heard of, if it came to that. With his weather-beaten face, wide teeth-crammed mouth, and far-seeing blue eyes, he looked like some wigwam warrior stained with suns and heroic slaughter. He spoke the Canadian dialect of the railway camps in a drawl through his resonant nose. His body was tattooed in every quarter—ships in full sail, flags of all nations, reptiles and round-eyed maidens. By cunning flexings of his muscled flesh he could sail those ships, wave the flags in the wind, and coil snakes round the quivering girls.

Laurie Lee introduces Uncle Ray dramatically—in the boy's bed snoring, a "huge and scaly man." The boy touches him, smells him, then the author proceeds to move the camera back for a more general description: who Ray is, where he's from, his physical attributes, his manner of speech—all authorially described. But Lee returns to dramatization in terms of the tattoos in motion, and the uncle's clever manipulation of them, all a part of a whole of description.

This is a description of the poet Octavius Coogan from Mary Temple's point of view in my novel *Separations*:

> "My Temple belles!" Octavius Coogan boomed, standing with his head ducked under the lintel of Mary's doorway. He carried a sheaf of white roses in one hand, a green magnum of champagne in the other. He was the tallest man Mary knew, with his auburn beard grown down to the third button of his shirtfront. He was clad in some version of a miner's garb—red shirt, blue jacket with brass buttons, blue trousers tucked into high boots. His face was broad and pink, with small, watchful eyes over a jib of a nose and wrinkled forehead beneath a sweep of stiff brown hair.

Coogan is based on the early California poet Joaquin Miller, a great poseur. He is just back from England where he impressed the literati with his homespun frontier bad verse and his personal style.

The following is also from *Separations*. Jake Buchanan is in charge of a Colorado River Expedition financed by the capitalist Charles P. Daggett. He has hoped Daggett would not accompany the expedition, which is in need of a cook. He draws his conclusions from what he observes:

> It wasn't a cook with Daggett, it was a sorry-looking mule skinner with a ragged hat.
>
> Daggett loved fancy dress, and his outfit lived up to expectations. The capitalist wore a dusty blue admiral's tunic with gold-braid epaulets, an admiral's fore-and-aft hat, and canvas leggings with brass trim. Buchanan ground his teeth at this evidence that Charley Daggett intended to come along on the expedition.
>
> He was aboard a long-eared mule. You could tell the mule skinner wasn't the cook because he was skinny as a rail and sour-looking, the two of them dusty all over.

4. Action

Action is a highly useful means of characterization. Character in action is what fiction is.

Here is Jewel with his horse, from Faulkner's *As I Lay Dying*. Brother Darl is observing:

> When Jewel can almost touch him, the horse stands on his hind legs and slashes down at Jewel. Then Jewel is enclosed by a glittering maze of hooves as by an illusion of wings; among them, beneath the upreared chest, he moves with the flashing limberness of a snake. For an instant before the jerk comes onto his arms he sees his whole body earth free, horizontal, whipping snake-limber, until he finds the horse's nostrils and touches earth again. Then they are rigid, motionless, terrific, the horse back-thrust on stiffened, quivering legs, with lowered head; Jewel with dug heels, shutting off the horse's wind with one hand, with the other patting the horse's neck in short strokes myriad and caressing, cursing the horse with obscene ferocity.
>
> They stand in rigid terrific hiatus, the horse trembling and groaning. Then Jewel is on the horse's back. He flows upward in a stooping swirl like the lash of a whip, his body in midair shaped to the horse. For another moment the horse stands spraddled, with lowered head, before it bursts into motion. They descend the hill in a series of spine-jolting jumps, Jewel high, leech-like on the withers, to the fence where the horse bunches to a scuttering halt again.
>
> "Well," Jewel says, "you can quit now, if you got a-plenty."
>
> Inside the barn Jewel slides running to the ground before the horse stops. The horse enters the stall, Jewel following. Without looking back the horse kicks at him, slamming a single hoof into the wall with a pistol-like report. Jewel kicks him in the stomach; the horse arches his back, crop-toothed; Jewel strikes him across the face with his fist and slides on to the trough and mounts upon it. Clinging to the hay-rack he lowers his head and peers out across the stall tops and through the doorway. The path is empty; from here he cannot even hear Cash sawing. He reaches up and drags down hay in hurried armsful and crams it into the rack.

"Eat," he says, "Get the goddamn stuff out of sight while you got a chance, you pussel-gutted bastard. You sweet son of a bitch," he says.

Jewel is defined in terms of his love for the horse, in action.

Here follows a characterization in action from MacDonald Harris's *Yukiko*. A team of commandos, including Havenmeyer, who is being observed by another member of the team, has landed on one of the northern Japanese islands:

> Havenmeyer is sitting on a rock . . . fieldstripping his .45 automatic to dry it and get the black volcanic sand out of it. He does this systematically. He has a cleaning rag which was sealed in a waterproof kit in the pack and is still dry. He spreads this out on a rock and sets the parts on it as he tears down the gun. First he slips out the magazine and removes the seven cartridges one by one, setting them in a neat row on the cloth. He peers in to be sure there isn't a round in the chamber, although he is reasonably sure there isn't. Then he presses on the plug under the muzzle to release the tension on the recoil spring, rotates the bushing to the right, and removes the plug and spring. Next the slide stop comes off, followed by the slide and its components. Conceivably these operations might be done in some other sequence, but he follows the drill. . . . Then he takes a small can of oil from the rock behind him and begins oiling each part in turn. . . . When he has oiled all the parts and wiped off the excess with the rag he reassembles it again, in reverse order. He pulls back the slide to see if it is working smoothly before he inserts the magazine, and not after.

We have a considerable grasp of Havenmeyer's character from the precision and drill of his fieldstripping of his .45, and his precautions. Havenmeyer will not shoot anyone accidentally, and he is a good man to have around in a pinch.

This is Muriel, from the J.D. Salinger story "A Great Day for Bananafish":

She was a girl who for a ringing phone dropped exactly nothing. She looked as if her phone had been ringing continually ever since she had reached puberty.

With her little lacquer brush, while the phone was ringing, she went over the nail of her little finger, accentuating the line of the moon. She then replaced the cap on the bottle of lacquer and, standing up, passed her left—the wet—hand back and forth through the air. With her dry hand, she picked up a congested ashtray from the window seat and carried it with her over to the night table, on which the telephone stood. She sat down on one of the made-up twin beds and—it was the fifth or sixth ring—picked up the phone.

Here is Miss Carmen Sternwood in action, from Raymond Chandler's *The Big Sleep*:

She put a thumb up and bit it. It was a curiously shaped thumb, thin and narrow like an extra finger, with no curve in the first joint. She bit and sucked it slowly, turning it around in her mouth like a baby with a comforter.

"You're awfully tall," she said. Then she giggled with a secret merriment. Then she turned her body slowly and lithely, without lifting her feet. Her hands dropped limp at her sides. She tilted herself toward me on her toes. She fell straight back into my arms. I had to catch her or let her crack her head on the tessellated floor. I caught her under the arms and she went rubber-legged on me instantly. I had to hold her close to hold her up. When her head was against my chest she screwed it around and giggled at me.

Philip Marlowe has a handful, or anyway an armful, here. How effective is the description of her thumb and how perverse her nursing on it. Her action of falling into his arms manipulates someone who is proud to think he cannot be manipulated. She is perverse, indulged, dangerous and, as it turns out, a murderess.

From Cormac McCarthy's *The Crossing*, here is more characterization through action:

> They rode the high country for weeks and they grew thin and gaunted man and horse and the horse grazed on the sparse winter grass in the mountains and gnawed lichens from the rock and the boy shot trout with his arrows where they stood above their shadows on the cold stone floors of the pools and he ate them and ate green nopal and then on a windy day traversing a high saddle in the mountains a hawk passed before the sun and its shadow ran so quick across the grass before them that it caused the horse to shy and the boy looked up where the bird turned high above them and he took an arrow from his shoulder and nocked and loosed the arrow and watched it rise with the wind rattling the fletching slotted into the cane and watched it turning and arcing and the hawk wheeling and then flaring suddenly with the arrow locked in its pale breast.
>
> The hawk turned and skated off down the wind and vanished behind the cape of the mountain, a single feather fell. He rode to look for it but he never found it. He found a single drop of blood that had dried on the rocks and darkened in the wind and nothing more. He dismounted and sat on the ground beside the horse where the wind blew and he made a cut in the heel of his hand with his knife and watched the slow blood dropping on the stone.

The boy, Spartan and morally righteous, punishes himself for his careless killing of the hawk, which dramatically illustrates his own nature, and his attitude toward nature.

5. Gestures and Mannerisms

Mr. Jaggers, the lawyer in Charles Dickens's *Great Expectations*, has a mannerism of biting his forefinger and flinging it toward whoever he is talking to, which is a repeated business and reinforces the readers' view of his domineering, bullying nature.

In Laurie Lee's *The Edge of Day*, Uncle Tom also has a repeated mannerism:

> Uncle Tom was well-mannered, something of a dandy, and he did peculiar things with his eyebrows. He could slide them independently up and down his forehead, and the habit was strangely suggestive. In moments of silence he did it constantly, as though to assure us he wished us well; and to this trick was ascribed much of his success with women. . . .

6. Setting, Taste and Interests

Madame Merle lectures Isabel Archer on the importance of *things*, in this speech from Henry James's *The Portrait of a Lady*:

> "When you've lived as long as I you'll see that every human has his shell and that you must take the shell into account. By the shell I mean the whole envelope of circumstances. There's no such thing as an isolated man or woman; we're each of us made up of some cluster of appurtenances. What shall we call our 'self'? Where does it begin? Where does it end? It over-flows into everything that belongs to us—and then it flows back again. I know a large part of myself is in the clothes I choose to wear. I've a great respect for *things*! One's self—for other people—is one's expression of one's self; and one's house, one's furniture, the books one reads, the company one keeps—these things are expressive."

Raymond Chandler presents General Sternwood's steamy quarters in *The Big Sleep*:

> The path took us along the side of the greenhouse and the butler opened a door for me and stood aside. It opened into a sort of vestibule that was about as warm as a slow oven. He came in after me, shut the outer door, opened an inner door and we went through that. Then it was really hot. The air was thick, wet, steamy and larded with the cloying smell of tropical orchids in bloom. The glass walls and roof were heavily misted and big

drops of moisture splashed down on the plants. The light had an unreal greenish color, like light filtered through an aquarium tank. The plants filled the place, a forest of them, with nasty meaty leaves and stalks like the newly washed fingers of dead men. They smelled as overpowering as boiling alcohol under a blanket.

The butler did his best to get me through without being smacked in the face by the sodden leaves, and after awhile we came into a clearing in the middle of the jungle, under the domed roof. Here, in a space of hexagonal flags, an old red Turkish rug was laid down and on the rug a wheelchair, and in the wheelchair an old and obviously dying man watched us come with black eyes from which all fire had died long ago. . . .

General Sternwood, with his petroleum fortune and his two daughters, one bad bad and one bad good, is so close to death, his vital fires burned so low, that he is like one of the hothouse orchids who can only live in this steamy atmosphere.

In this paragraph from the novel *The Magician's Tale* by David Hunt, the narrator, Kay, and her journalist friend Joel have gone to call on a retired police detective, Hale, who has spent his retirement obsessively trying to solve the case that has been his downfall as a cop. Here we see Hale's den as his character:

As he and Joel feel each other out, I make a quick study of the room. At first glance it appears ordinary, a den outfitted with recycled office furniture, books, framed nostalgia photographs, clippings and awards. But after a minute I feel claustrophobic, and then it occurs to me that the room is not only windowless but also cramped. There's too much in here, too many old clippings clustered on the walls, too many books jammed into the bookcases, too many moldy boxes of files strewn upon the threadbare rug. And, too, it seems ill proportioned, depth insufficient to width. Perhaps, I think, it's a metaphor for Hale's mind.

7. Others' Opinions

The following passage is from George Eliot's *Middlemarch.* George Eliot is of the Great Tradition of the English novel before Henry James's ideas of "centers of consciousness" began to replace the old omniscience. This passage is authorial, but Eliot knows that her description of Dorothea Brooke will be dramatized by the point of view of the two painters who observe her and that their impressions will validate Dorothea's beauty more effectively than the author's assertions:

> One fine morning a young man whose hair was not immoderately long, but abundant and curly, and who was otherwise English in his equipment, had just turned his back on the Belvedere Torso in the Vatican and was looking out on the magnificent view of the mountains from the adjoining vestibule. He was sufficiently absorbed not to notice the approach of a dark-eyed, animated German who came up to him and placing a hand on his shoulder, said with a strong accent, "Come here, quick! Else she will have changed her pose."
>
> Quickness was ready at the call, and the two figures passed lightly along by the Meleager towards the hall where the reclining Ariadne, then called the Cleopatra, lies in the marble voluptuousness of her beauty, the drapery folding around her with a petal-like ease and tenderness. They were just in time to see another figure standing against a pedestal near the reclining marble: a breathing, blooming girl, whose form, not shamed by the Ariadne, was clad in Quakerish grey drapery; her long cloak, fastened at the neck, was thrown backward from her arms, and one beautiful ungloved hand pillowed her cheek, pushing somewhat backward the white beaver bonnet which made a sort of halo to her face around the simply braided dark-brown hair. She was not looking at the sculpture, probably not thinking of it: her large eyes were fixed dreamily on a streak of sunlight that fell across the floor. But she became conscious of the two strangers who suddenly paused as if to contemplate the Cleopatra, and, without looking at them, immediately turned

away to join a maid-servant and courier who were loitering along the hall at a little distance off.

"What do you think of that for a fine bit of antithesis?" said the German, searching his friend's face for responding admiration, but going on voluably without waiting for any other answer. "There lies antique beauty, not corpse-like even in death, but arrested in the complete contentment of its sensuous perfection: and here stands beauty in its breathing life, with the consciousness of Christian centuries in its bosom. But she should be dressed as a nun; I think she looks almost what you call a Quaker; I would dress her as a nun in my picture. However, she is married; I saw her wedding-ring on that wonderful left hand. . . ."

George Eliot has the German artist make the point of Dorothea's nunlike beauty contrasted to the sensuous beauty of the sculpture, knowing it is stronger coming from a character in the fiction than from the author. Dorothea's nunlikeness says something of her relation with her new husband, Casaubon. The younger artist, Will Ladislaw, who is Casaubon's cousin, is struck dumb because he will fall in love with Dorothea, and she, ultimately, with him.

In the novel *Birdsong* by Sebastian Faulks, Stephen is a young Englishman resident with a French couple, in France, on business. He is becoming sexually obsessed with the wife, whom he feels may be abused by her husband, and he keeps a notebook in which he conceals real names in code words:

In his notebook the code word Stephen used when describing a certain aspect of Madame Azaire and of his confused feeling towards her was "pulse." It seemed to him to be sufficiently cryptic, yet also to suggest something of his suspicion that she was animated by a different kind of rhythm from that which beat in her husband's blood. It also referred to an unusual aspect of her physical presence. No one could have been more proper in her dress and her toilet than Madame Azaire. She spent long parts of the day bathing or changing her clothes, she carried a light scent of rose soap or perfume when she brushed past him in the passageways. Her clothes were more fashionable than those of other women in the town yet revealed less. She carried herself modestly when she sat or stood, she slid into chairs with her feet close together, so that beneath the folds of her skirt her knees too must have been almost touching. When she rose again it was without any leverage from her hands or arms but with a spontaneous upward movement of grace and propriety. Her white hands seemed barely to touch the cutlery when they ate at the family dinner table and her lips left no trace of their presence on the wine glass. On one occasion, Stephen noticed, some tiny adhesion caused the membrane of her lower lip to linger for a fraction of a second as she pulled the glass away to return it to its place, but still the surface of it had remained clear and shining. She caught him staring at it.

Yet despite her formality toward him and her punctilious ease of manner, Stephen sensed some other element in what he had termed the pulse of her. It was impossible to say through which sense he had the impression, but somehow, perhaps only in the tiny white hairs on the skin of her bare arm or the blood he had seen rise beneath the light freckles of her cheekbones, he felt certain there was some keener physical life than she was actually living in the calm, restrictive rooms of her husband's house with its oval door handles of polished china and its neatly inlaid parquet floors.

Much of Madame Azaire's physical presence is revealed here by the author, with whatever character it implies, perhaps more of a desire for more knowledge on the part of the reader than knowledge itself. It is the incisiveness of Stephen's vision of her that characterizes him. He is watching this woman very closely, and the intensity and the quality of his assessment of her tells us much about him.

A device commonly used by writers of popular fiction is the introduction of a character merely for the purpose of observing the protagonist, for the reader's benefit. Such is the use of the Wren Officer, who is interviewing the protagonist in *The Shell Seekers* by Rosamunde Pilcher. Penelope has enlisted in the Wrens at the beginning of World War II. The terms of the officer's disapproval are effective in gaining reader sympathy for Penelope, for the terms of this disapproval appeal to the reader and help develop interest in the character:

> "Have you any qualifications?"
> "No, I don't think so."
> "Shorthand? Typing?"
> "No."
> "University degree?"
> "No."
> "You must call me 'Ma'am.' "
> "Ma'am."
> The Wren Officer cleared her throat, finding herself discon-
> certed by the guileless expression and dreamy brown eyes of
> the new Wren Rating. She wore uniform, but somehow it didn't
> look right on her; she was too tall, and her legs were too long,
> and her hair was a disaster, soft and dark and bundled up into
> a loose coil that looked neither safe nor secure.

Penelope has been characterized by the officer's critical attention of her appearance.

Here is another example of viewpoint disapproval that gives an opposite effect. This is a passage from Iain Pears's *An Instance of the Fingerpost*. The narrator, Marco da Cola, a Venetian gentleman, is giving his opinion of a young Englishwoman. The reader disagrees. In fact the reader may become more interested in the character just because he finds the judgment offered him to be (rather transparently) mistaken or prejudiced.

> A brief glance disclosed a woman of, I suppose, about nineteen
> or twenty years of age, of average height but unnaturally slim
> of build: none of the plumpness that endows true Beauty. . . .
> Her hair was dark and had only natural curls in it, her clothes
> were drab (though well cared for) and, while she was pretty
> enough in the face, there was nothing obviously exceptional

about her. Even so, she was one of those people whom you look at, turn away from, then somehow find yourself looking at once more.

Marco da Cola is interested in this young woman despite his negative first impression, and so is the reader.

In *The Portrait of a Lady*, Isabel Archer at first appears to readers a little too cool, snippy, collected and opinionated, but because they have come to like and respect Ralph Touchett, and he admires his cousin, readers are persuaded to like her, also.

8. Dialogue

One of the most effective means of presenting character is in that character's own words. This is the first page of Doris Betts's novel *The Sharp Teeth of Love*. Notice the efficient and effective characterization of Steven, and of Luna's attitude toward him:

> Luna had been holding her small open diary, indecisive, for too long above two boxes of last-minute things to keep or throw away, when something in her uncertain swaying made her recall that illustration from an old textbook: an emaciated donkey unable to choose between two equal hay bales, above the caption "Dilemma."
>
> She opened the book to its blank page for today, and wrote in the date, April 6, 1993. In fact, since she'd left the hospital, almost all the pages were blank.
>
> The minute Steven came in, she threw it in the Keeper Box. Naturally he picked up that box to load into the van, leaving her to drag the heavier one to their curbside trash. She could feel her face, perhaps even her brain, take on the prune surface of petulance.
>
> He climbed behind the steering wheel, whistling, while she made one last check of the bare rooms, unplugged the refrigerator, left the door key under the empty flowerpot as promised.
>
> "Did you get film for my camera?" he asked as she got into the van.

For answer, she opened the glove compartment to show him the yellow boxes.

Charles Baxter, in his story "Gryphon," characterizes the interesting Miss Ferenczi, the substitute teacher:

We were doing multiplication tables. Miss Ferenczi had made John Wazny stand up at his desk in the front row. He was supposed to go through the tables of six. I could smell the Vitalis soaked into John's plastered hair. He was doing fine until he came to six times eleven and six times twelve. "Six times eleven," he said, "is sixty-eight. Six times twelve is . . ." He put his fingers to his head, quickly and secretly sniffed his fingertips, and said, "seventy-two." Then he sat down.

"Fine," Miss Ferenczi said. "Well now. That was very good."

"Miss Ferenczi!" One of the Eddy twins was waving her hand desperately in the air. "Miss Ferenczi! Miss Ferenczi!"

"Yes?"

"John said that six times eleven is sixty-eight and you said he was right!"

"*Did* I?" She gazed at the class with a jolly look breaking across her marionette's face. "Did I say that? Well, what is six times eleven?"

"It's sixty-six!"

She nodded. "Yes. So it is. But, and I know some people will not entirely agree with me, at some times it is sixty-eight."

"When? When is it sixty-eight?"

We were all waiting.

"In higher mathematics, which you children do not yet understand, six times eleven can be considered to be sixty-eight." She laughed through her nose. "In higher mathematics numbers are. . . more fluid. The only thing a number does is contain a certain amount of something. Think of water. A cup is not the only way to measure a certain amount of water, is it?" We were staring, shaking our heads. "You could use saucepans or thimbles. In either case, the water *would be the same*. Perhaps," she started again, "it would be better for you to think that six times eleven is sixty-eight only when I am in the room."

"Why is it sixty-eight," Mark Poole said, "when you're in the room?"

"Because it's more interesting that way," she said, smiling very rapidly behind her blue-tinted glasses. "Besides, I'm your substitute teacher, am I not?" We all nodded. "Well, then, think of six times eleven equals sixty-eight as a substitute fact."

John O'Hara, in his story "Mrs. Allanson," gives us essential information as to the characters of Mrs. Allanson, a small-minded society widow, and her daughter, all in dialogue. It should be noted that character is revealed in dialogue most effectively in contention:

"Mother?"

Sara Allanson did not turn. "Yes?"

"I'm sorry I was rude."

"Well, I should think you would be. Where did you sleep?"

"In the attic."

"In the *attic*?"

"In the old playroom."

"Why? What did you sleep *on*? There's no bed made up."

"I know. I'm stiff. I slept on the floor."

"Why? What made you do that?"

"I don't know. I just did."

"Well, you had better get yourself a hot bath or you'll be stiff the rest of the day. I see you haven't changed your dress."

"I know."

"I was just going down to breakfast. What do you want? And rumple your bed. I don't want Agnes to think you stayed out all night."

"Mother, I don't *care* what Agnes thinks."

"I'm sure you don't, but I do."

"But I wish you didn't."

"You have to care what people think in this world."

"I don't."

"Well, you'd better start."

"It's too late for me to start."

So we know a good deal about square Mrs. Allanson and her honest daughter.

In Martha McPhee's *Bright Angel Time*, the mother and father are separated and the mother and her three girls are travelling in a camper with the mother's lover. Information that would not have come out in normal conversation is blurted in a fight:

"Shut up, Julia!" I spat.

"Don't start, Kate," Mom said, glaring back at me. I noticed little wrinkles were appearing beneath her eyes.

"I'm not starting anything."

"Don't be selfish, Kate. Grow up," Jane said, turning to glare at me. That was her new thing, don't be selfish. Grow up. She was perched in the front, cheek pressed close to Mom's, as if she and Mom were one, acting like mothers together. It made me mad.

"Why can't we stay in the motel?" I said. "We always used to stay in hotels. Normal people stay in hotels. Dad stays in hotels."

"You're being a child," Jane said.

"I am not being a child," I yelled.

"Oh, come off it," Julia said to both of us.

But then Mom's voice turned as sharp as a slap. "If you think *he's* so *normal*, then go home. It's his fault, Kate. He didn't give me a chance, Kate. He's cheated *us*, Kate." She got out of the car and slammed the door.

The reiteration of the name *Kate* is especially effective in Mom's sudden rant and disclosure of the wrongs done her.

In the film *When Harry Met Sally . . .* , one line of dialogue, in fact one joking epithet, tells us a great deal about Sally, and about Harry's attitude toward Sally, and so about Harry, too. He refers to her as "Miss Hospital-corners."

9. Thoughts, Interiorization

The sixteen-year-old Lara has a moment of introspection in Pasternak's *Doctor Zhivago*. She has been kissed by her mother's lover and perceives the danger of her situation. As with Shakespearean soliloquies, her introspection ends with a decision for action:

> She would never have dreamed there could be so much effrontery in anyone's lips when they were pressed for such a long time against her own.
>
> She must stop all this nonsense. Once and for all. Stop playing at being shy, simpering and lowering her eyes—or it would end in disaster. There loomed an imperceptible, a terrifying border-line. One step and you would be hurtled into an abyss. . . .

Here is Sue Grafton's private eye in *H Is for Homicide* up early and on the 405 freeway en route home:

> I always feel an affinity for others traveling at such an hour, as if we are all engaged in some form of clandestine activity. Many of the other drivers had oversize Styrofoam cups of coffee. Some were actually managing to wolf down fast food as they drove. With the occasional car window rolled down, I was treated to bursts of booming music that faded away as the cars passed me, changing lanes. A glance in my rearview mirror showed a woman in the convertible behind me emoting with vigor, belting out a lip-sync solo as the wind whipped through her hair. I felt a jolt of pure joy. It was one of those occasions when I suddenly realized how happy I was. Life was good. I was female, single, with money in my pocket and enough gas to get home. I had nobody to answer to and no ties to speak of. I was healthy, physically fit, filled with energy. I flipped on the radio and chimed in on a chorus of "Amazing Grace," which

didn't quite suit the occasion but was the only station I could find. An early morning evangelist began to make his pitch, and by the time I reached Ventura, I was nearly redeemed. As usual, I'd forgotten how often surges of goodwill merely presage bad news.

This paragraph not only dramatizes the heroine's good spirits, it informs readers of her character and situation in life. She is possessed of joy, she is healthy and single and has enough gas to get home. But reality rings a warning bell, and readers know full well (since this is a mystery novel) that her goodwill presages bad news.

10. All of the Above

For the greatest effect in characterization, many methods and uses will be employed in combinations, as in the following section from Anne Tyler's *The Accidental Tourist*. Macon Leary's first meeting with Muriel Pritchett is a tour de force of character revelation. Macon is departing for a brief European trip and must deposit his dog Edward at a pet hospital while he is gone:

> MEOW-BOW ANIMAL HOSPITAL, a sign across the street read. Macon braked and Edward lurched forward. "Sorry," Macon told him. He made a left turn into the parking lot.
>
> The waiting room at the Meow-Bow smelled strongly of disinfectant. Behind the counter stood a thin young woman in a ruffled peasant blouse. She had aggressively frizzy black hair that burgeoned to her shoulders like an Arab headress. "Hey, there," she said to Macon.
>
> Macon said, "Do you board dogs?"
>
> "Sure."
>
> "I'd like to board Edward, here."
>
> She leaned over the counter to look at Edward. Edward panted up at her cheerfully. It was clear he hadn't yet realized what kind of a place this was.
>
> "You have a reservation?" the woman asked Macon.
>
> "Reservation! No."

"Most people reserve."

"Well, I didn't know that."

"Especially in the summer."

"Couldn't you make an exception?"

She thought it over, frowning down at Edward. Her eyes were very small, like caraway seeds, and her face was sharp and colorless.

"Please," Macon said. "I'm about to catch a plane. I'm leaving for a week, and I don't have a soul to look after him. I'm desperate, I tell you."

From the glance she shot him, he sensed he had surprised her in some way. "Can't you leave him home with your wife?" she asked.

He wondered how her mind worked.

"If I could do that," he said, "why would I be standing here?"

"Oh," she said. "You're not married?"

"Well, I am, but she's . . . living elsewhere. They don't allow pets."

"Oh."

She came out from behind the counter. She was wearing very short red shorts; her legs were like sticks. "I'm a divorsy myself," she said. "I know what you're going through."

"And see," Macon said, "there's this place I usually board him but they claim he bites. Claim he bit an attendant and they can't admit him anymore."

"Edward? Do you bite?" the woman said.

Macon realized he should not have mentioned that, but she seemed to take it in stride. "How could you do such a thing?" she asked Edward. Edward grinned up at her and folded his ears back, inviting a pat. She bent and stroked his head.

"So will you keep him?" Macon asked.

"Oh, I guess," she said, straightening. "If you're desperate." She stressed the word—fixing Macon with those small brown eyes—as if giving it more weight than he had intended.

"Fill this out," she told him, and she handed him a form from a stack on the counter. "Your name and address and when you'll be back. Don't forget to put when you'll be back."

Macon nodded, uncapping his fountain pen.

"I'll most likely see you again when you come to pick him up," she said. "I mean if you put the time of day to expect you. My name's Muriel."

"Is this place open evenings?" Macon asked.

"Every evening but Sundays. Till eight."

"Oh, good."

"Muriel Pritchett," she said.

The characterizations here are in terms of description, action and dialogue. The author has employed vivid details to present Muriel: her frizzy hair, her short shorts and stick legs, her small brown eyes. She is shown in action. There is a nice contrast with Macon's name for his dog, Edward, and hers for her pet hospital, the Meow-Bow. Her use of the term *divorsy*, not one that Macon would ever enunciate, is revealing, and her interest in Macon is evident. The reader is certain that she will be on hand at the appointed hour of his return.

Shading

Tolstoy employed a method of characterization that he termed "shading," building a character out of contradictions. A coldhearted character would be first presented in a state of passion so that the reader could then have the pleasure of discovering that that was not the true character. When the reader first meets General Kutosov, in *War and Peace*, he speaks calmly of the destruction of a detachment of soldiers. Prince Andrey considers this justified because of the general's great responsibilities. Later the reader learns of Kutosov's overwhelming compassion for his men, which provides a dramatic enlargement of the understanding of him.

Anne Tyler is using a similar device in the above passage from *The Accidental Tourist*. Muriel Pritchett is described in unfavorable terms, from Macon Leary's point of view. She has a kind of Arab's headdress of hair, her legs are like sticks, her eyes like caraway seeds, her face sharp and white. She uses language that must be painful to the proper Macon. But as the novel progresses Macon comes to have a very different view of Muriel, who will change his life.

The Page-Turner Consideration

The following passage is from Michael Crichton's *Rising Sun*. A central character is an American cop, Peter Smith:

> Actually I was sitting on my bed in my apartment in Culver City, watching the Lakers game with the sound turned off, while I tried to study vocabulary for my introductory Japanese class.
>
> It was a quiet evening, I had gotten my daughter to sleep about eight. Now I had the cassette player on the bed, and the cheerful woman's voice was saying things like "Hello, I am a police officer. Can I be of assistance?" and "Please show me the menu."

There is a lot of information here, very specific. The fact that the subject is a policeman already creates some tension; things happen to policemen. He lives in Culver City, in an apartment, not a house. He's a Lakers fan (very L.A.). He's taking a Japanese course, which is an interesting aspect of a policeman. He has a young daughter, and there is no mother in evidence. This is not exactly characterization, but many of these details make us want a more complete characterization. Why, for instance, is an L.A. cop taking a course in Japanese? Why does he have the TV sound turned off? Because his daughter is asleep? Or perhaps because there is a wife who is an invalid in the bedroom? Are these phrases from the Japanese tapes hints as to what the novel is about? These are the page-turner aspects of Michael Crichton's novels, which are his great strength.

There was a similar page-turner detail about the girl Luna in the excerpt from *The Sharp Teeth of Love* on page 124—that she is recently out of the hospital.

Character as Plot

Here follow examples from two contemporary novels in which characters reveal themselves in action, and also set the plot in motion by their personal qualities.

In *Princess Daisy,* Judith Krantz introduces her heroine in action, atop the Empire State Building:

> "We could always shoot this on top of the RCA Building," Daisy said, walking past the parapet, above which rose a high, metal railing designed to forestall would-be suicides. "They're not nearly as paranoid as you Empire State people." She gestured scornfully at the ledge behind her. "But, Mr. Jones, the message just won't be New York."
>
> The man in uniform watched, motionless in surprise, as Daisy suddenly leapt high and held on to a rung of the railing with one strong hand. With the other hand she took off the sailor hat under which she had tucked her hair and let it blow free. The silver-gilt tumble was caught by the breeze that separated it into a million brave and dazzling threads.
>
> "Come down, Miss," the man in charge of the Observation Deck begged. "I told you it's just not allowed. . . . You can't go up there. You didn't tell me you wanted to the last time you came," he reproached her, circling cautiously closer. "It's never permitted. It could be dangerous."
>
> "But all great art has to break rules," Daisy called down to him gaily.

Daisy's action, more effectively than her words, shows that she likes to flout rules. She is an ambitious TV producer. She is high, atop the Empire State Building, but she wants to climb higher still, despite rules and dangers. She is daring, fearless, practiced at getting what she wants, sometimes scornful. Judith Krantz wants the reader to be fascinated by her high-flying heroine and shows her in action in order to catch the eye, and it is these traits of Daisy's that will drive the plotline.

The next passage is from Maeve Binchy's *Circle of Friends*. Benny, the heroine, has just had a birthday party to which, on a whim, she has invited Eve, an orphan who is being brought up by nuns. Eve has come to the party inappropriately dressed. She and Benny are in conversation when Maire Carroll intrudes:

Eve was about to reply when Maire Carroll came by.

"That was a nice party, Benny," she said.

"Thanks."

"I didn't know it was meant to be fancy dress though."

"What do you mean?" Benny asked.

"Well, Eve was in fancy dress, weren't you, Eve? I mean that big red thing, that wasn't meant to be ordinary clothes was it?"

Eve's face tightened into that hard look that she used to have before. Benny hated to see that expression come back.

"I thought it was quite funny myself," Maire said with a little laugh. "We all did when we were coming home."

Benny looked around the school yard. Mother Francis was looking the other way.

With all her strength Benny Hogan launched herself off the wall down on Maire Carroll. The girl fell over, winded.

"Are you all right Maire?" Benny asked, in a falsely sympathetic tone.

Mother Francis came running, her habit streaming behind her.

"What happened child?" She was struggling to get Maire's breath back, and raise her to her feet.

"Benny pushed me . . ." Maire gasped.

"Mother, I'm sorry, I'm so clumsy, I was just getting off the wall."

"All right, all right, no bones broken. Get her a stool." Mother Francis dealt with the panting Maire.

"She did it purposely."

"Shush, shush, Maire. Here's a little stool for you, sit down now."

Maire was crying. "Mother, she just jumped down from the

wall on me like a ton of bricks . . . I was only saying . . ."

"Maire was telling me how much she liked the party Mother. I'm so sorry," Benny said.

"Yes, well Benny, try to be more careful. Don't throw yourself around so much. Now, Maire, enough of this whining. It's not a bit nice. Benny has said she was sorry. You know it was an accident. Come along now and be a big girl."

"I'd never want to be as big a girl as Benny Hogan. No one would."

Mother Francis was cross now. "That's quite enough, Maire Carroll. Quite enough. Take that stool and go inside to the cloakroom and sit there until you're called by me to come away from it."

Mother Francis swept away. And as they all knew she would, she rang the bell for the end of break.

Eve looked at Benny. For a moment she said nothing, she just swallowed as if there was a lump in her throat.

Benny was equally at a loss, she just shrugged and spread her hands helplessly.

Suddenly Eve grasped her hand. "Someday, when I'm big and strong, I'll knock someone down for you," she said. "I mean it, I really will."

Here is characterization turning into plot, as already seen in the Observation Platform scene from *Princess Daisy*. Benny has displayed a largeness of spirit in her assault on Maire Carroll, and Eve has announced that she will repay the favor in kind. This is a promise not merely from Eve to Benny but from the author to the reader, and a plotline is set up.

The following passage is from Flaubert's *Madame Bovary*, and is a scene from the courtship of Charles Bovary and Emma Roualt. Admirable in this scene is the fact that all the description is given in terms of action, and Emma characterized in one short take:

> One day he arrived at the farm about three o'clock. Everybody was out in the fields. He went into the kitchen, and at first failed to notice Emma; the shutters were closed. Through the chinks

in the wood the sunshine came streaking across the floor in long slender lines that broke at the corners of the furniture and flickered on the ceiling. Flies were crawling over the dirty glasses on the table, buzzing as they drowned themselves in the dregs of cider. Daylight came down the chimney, laying a velvet sheen on the soot of the fireplace and tinging the cold ashes with blue. Emma sat between the window and the hearth, sewing. She had nothing round her neck, and little drops of perspiration stood on her bare shoulders.

In accordance with country customs, she offered him a drink. He declined. She pressed him. Finally she suggested with a laugh that they should take a liqueur together. She fetched a bottle of curaçao from the cupboard, reached down two small glasses, filled one to the brim, poured the merest drop into the other, and, after clinking glasses, raised hers to her lips. As there was practically nothing in it, she tilted her head right back to drink. With her head back and her lips rounded and the skin of her neck stretched tight, she laughed at her own vain efforts, and slid the tip of her tongue between her fine teeth to lick, drop by drop, the bottom of the glass.

Flaubert has shown Emma's nature in this action. She is impatient with the paltry portion of liquor, and the portion of life that is her share. Her sensuality is shown in the manner in which her tongue explores the bottom of her glass. Her future and her tragedy are indicated.

Henry James introduces the reader to a group of men gathered on the lawn of an English country house and the young woman, Isabel Archer, who is to "affront her destiny" as the protagonist of the novel *The Portrait of a Lady*:

Ralph Touchett wandered away a little, with his usual slouching gait, his hands in his pockets, and his little rowdyish terrier at his heels. His face was turned toward the house, but his eyes were bent musingly on the lawn; so that he had been an object of observation to a person who had just made her appearance in the ample doorway for some moments before he perceived her. His attention was called to her by the conduct of his dog, who had suddenly darted forward with a little volley of shrill barks, in which the note of welcome, however, was more sensible than that of defiance. The person in question was a young lady, who seemed immediately to interpret the greeting of the small beast. He advanced with great rapidity and stood at her feet, looking up and barking hard; whereupon, without hesitation, she stooped and caught him in her hands, holding him face to face while he continued his quick chatter. His master now had time to follow and to see that Bunchie's new friend was a tall girl in a black dress, who at first sight looked pretty. She was bareheaded. . . .

Isabel is quick on the uptake, trusting and unafraid, and unconventional (her bareheadedness). These are the qualities that interest Ralph Touchett, and the reader, in her. They are also the qualities that will prove her undoing, for in old, corrupt Europe one cannot be so trusting that one will not be bitten. She affronts her destiny by allowing herself to be suckered by Madame Merle into marrying Gilbert Osmond, who clips the wings Ralph Touchett had meant to set free by providing her with a fortune. Her actions reveal her character and her character fuels the plot.

The narrative voice in Raymond Chandler's novel *The Long Goodbye* is Philip Marlowe, on the surface a hard-boiled and cynical private eye but essentially a romantic, bound by a strict code of honor. This scene is the end of the novel. Terry Lennox is leaving Marlowe's office and his life. They have been friends. The draft versions are from Frank MacShane's *The Life of Raymond Chandler*. This is an early draft of the last paragraph:

He turned away and went out. I watched the door close and listened to his steps going away. After a little while, I couldn't hear them, but I kept on listening. Don't ask me why. I couldn't tell you.

Here is the rewrite:

He turned and went out. I watched the door close and listened to his steps going away. Then I couldn't hear them, but I kept on listening anyway. As if he might come back and talk me out of it, as if I hoped he would.

But he didn't.

Chandler is striving for a Hemingway ending here, as in *A Farewell to Arms*—". . . I walked back to the hotel in the rain"—Frederick Henry's thoughts and emotions so terrible in his grief at the death of his lover that they cannot be expressed, and are the more powerful for the expression not being attempted.

Here is Chandler's final version:

> He turned and walked across the floor and out. I watched the door close. I listened to his steps going away down the imitation marble corridor. After awhile they got faint, then they got silent. I kept on listening, anyway. What for? Did I want him to stop suddenly and turn and come back and talk me out of the way I felt? Well, he didn't. That was the last I saw of him.

Chandler has found Marlowe's authentic tone of cynicism failing to conceal a depth of emotion.

Michael Ondaatje has this to say of character:

> I'm always accused of being plotless. Plot is discovered as I go along, in the writing. For me plot isn't event the way it is, say, in a Mickey Spillane novel—all of which I read when I was a kid. He knocks off 18 people and, as he goes from one to 18, you're following along. But you don't really discover anything more about the depth of character.
>
> Plot can be about that as well—the discovery of character, the unearthing of a relationship.

First Aid for Character

1. Make sure the character has a physical presence, leaves footprints in the damp grass, breathes, has a smell, etc.
2. Sharpen the character's sensory perceptions, and give those perceptions an individualistic slant.

3. Rewrite all the character's lines of dialogue serially to keep them keyed to the character and expressive of it.

4. If the character is the point-of-view character, change from first person to third, or vice versa. (You will get a slightly to considerably different character.)

5. Sharpen motivations and compulsions.

6. Arrange scenes so that other characters are conscious of, and have opinions on, the character in question, in dialogue or point of view.

CHAPTER 8

Plot

All human happiness and misery take the form of action.

—ARISTOTLE, *THE POETICS*

Plot at best is essence, story, action, the purpose of a narrative work, the means by which it conveys what it wishes to say, the method of arousing expectations and providing fulfillment, presenting anticipations, possibilities and resolutions.

Plot at worst is formula, skeleton, mechanism, contrivance and the cheapest trickery, of the kind that promises more than can be delivered.

Plot is the dynamic aspect of narrative, a progressive line of energies and tensions, compulsions, resistances and desires, that holds the promise of ultimately delivering meaning and satisfaction.

Plot is what especially distinguishes popular mass-market fiction; plot is why we read popular fiction but not literature.

Plot can thus be viewed as noble or merely mechanical. It can in fact be either, and the fiction writer had better be aware that he must deal with it in that duality.

Writers who are too fastidious to deal with plot because of its low reputation, humiliating demands and general frowziness turn to character as the alternative. Their novels become character studies, with, often, *Portrait* in the title, or implied. In these the reader should not expect much action and should look for resolution in the completion of a pattern, or the portrait, rather than change and stasis achieved in the fictional lives.

The novelist's distrust of (or laziness about) plot is what has made the general public turn away from the "literary" novel.

An editor friend of mine claims that 90 percent of first novels fail on deficiencies of plot.

These jacket quotes will tell us something about character vs. plot in the enclosed pages. This from *The Saskiad* by Brian Hall:

> A delightful coming of age novel—richly detailing one girl's fantastic search for her place in her own epic history.

Or this from *Five Minutes in Heaven* by Lisa Alther:

> . . . follows a young girl named Jude—haunted by dreams, ghosts and longings—on an epic search for love, intimacy and answers to questions she cannot forget.

It would appear that these are novels of character where plot is merely paid lip service by the term *epic*.

Strong plots (as well as strong characters) is the reason classic Victorian novels turn up in new brilliantly costumed TV and theatrical films year after year.

It may be well here to mention the old saw that men believe that women will never change while women believe that men will change (or can be changed), and both are wrong.

Change, however, is the basis of plot.

Again we can say there are two kinds of plot:

1. the plot of action, in which the *situation* of the protagonist is changed
2. the plot of character, in which the *character* of the protagonist is changed

Subdivisions to the Plot of Character

1. **The Maturing Plot**: The protagonist's goals are either mistaken or undetermined, or vacillating. Means must be devised for giving the character strength and direction. This may be accomplished through some drastic, even fatal misfortune, such as the convict revealing himself as Pip's benefactor in *Great Expectations*, or Lord Jim

accepting death to prove his regained strength and purpose. The Maturing Plot is often a coming-of-age (maturing) of young people.

2. **The Reformation Plot**: A bad character reforms due to plot forces brought to bear, such as Scrooge in *A Christmas Carol.*

3. **The Test Plot**: A weak or vacillating character is enabled to pass some major life test, such as the young soldier in *The Red Badge of Courage* or any number of other fictional soldiers, or, often, a lawyer on a slippery slope of liquor or morals.

4. **The Degeneration Plot**: This is a kind of opposite of the Maturing Plot, in which the protagonist disintegrates in terms (usually) of drink, drugs or existential despair, such as the protagonists of *The Lost Weekend* or *Lie Down in Darkness.*

Character and plot tend to separate into distinct genres in the contemporary novel. Literary works get the characters; adventure stories the plots.

In the plot of action interest is caught by what happens next and characters are portrayed minimally in terms of the necessities required to forward the action. The pleasures the reader experiences are those of suspense, expectation and surprise.

In a plot of action the protagonist marries the beautiful girl, becomes president of the company, saves the world from nuclear destruction, returns safely from the dangerous confrontation or is killed. In any case, his situation is changed.

The plot of character is more likely to be a literary novel. The protagonist realizes he still loves his wife and takes steps to rectify his past mistakes, comes to understand his son's difficulties with the gangs at school and establishes a new relationship with him, or changes from an arrogant and violent detective into a good guy and proves it. Or vice versa.

Plots can of course be *both* of action and of character, with a change in situation as well as in moral character. Insofar as character or any other element in narrative is dynamic, it is part of the plot.

In his important book *Aspects of the Novel*, E.M. Forster makes the distinction between story and plot that I will paraphrase here as a distinction between the plot of action and the plot of character:

> The Queen died, no one knew why, until it was discovered that
> it was through grief at the death of the King. . . . Consider the
> death of the Queen. If it is a story (*say, an action plot*) we say
> "and then?" If it is a plot (*a character plot*) we ask "why?"
> (Emphasis added)

In *Great Expectations*, a young boy, Pip, of humble circumstances, with the help of an anonymous benefactor makes himself into a moneyed gentleman in order to prove himself worthy of a handsome and wealthy girl with whom he has fallen in love. In the process, however, Pip becomes a worthless snob who is ashamed of his old friends and haunts, until the convict who, in secret, has given him the money to establish his gentleman's status, reveals himself. The shock of this discovery causes Pip to change. He sees what he has become, and makes amends by returning in humility to his old home and friends.

A secondary plot is that of a bitter old woman who was jilted on her wedding day and has brought up her beautiful niece Estella to take revenge on men for the wrongs the aunt has suffered. It is Estella with whom Pip is in love. Dickens first ended the novel with Pip losing Estella, but, advised by his friend Bulwer-Lytton that this would disappoint his public, he changed the ending to a happy one.

The successful function of plot lies in the synthesis of character and action that moves our feelings powerfully and pleasurably. An ideal plot would present a hero who is particular because of a tragic flaw, a peculiar strength, a singular aptitude or vulnerability that causes a hypothetical snowball to form and grow and roll down a steep hill, where it smashes the protagonist flat but produces in him a change of character and of fortune.

The writer should have combined action and character so as to have achieved an ordered whole, with all the parts needed to carry the protagonist, by probable and necessary stages, from the beginning to the end of the character change.

What kind of person is the protagonist? Do we fear his/her fortunes will become worse, or do we hope they will become better? Do we feel he/she is sufficiently aware of the facts of the situation and the consequences of his/her behavior in order to bear responsibility for what he/she does and undergoes? And do the essential forces of cause and effect bring about his/her change?

Character change is revealed when the protagonist decides voluntarily to pursue or abandon a course of action, and in showing that decision in effect.

In general we are more convinced and moved when things are rendered, shown through character and action, rather than merely given in statement, after the fashion of a scenario.

The Uses of Myths and Models

In Louis B. Jones's novel *California's Over,* early on the protagonist encounters a coffeehouse called Little Tom's Round Table. Further along he tries unsuccessfully to draw a pen from its holder. The reader has been warned that Arthurian myth is engaged and she had better start looking for the Holy Grail. This proves to be a dead poet's "cremains," or perhaps his lost last manuscript, or else a defunct casino in Nevada in search of which a number of the characters ride out on a quest.

The use of Arthurian symbolism is not essential to the plot but reinforces it.

In Charles Frazier's Pulitzer prize–winning novel, *Cold Mountain*, the hero, Inman, departs from the Civil War headed home, where a woman who may be his beloved waits. The journey home is certainly an odyssey, the woman Ada a kind of Penelope. Inman's adventures do not much resemble those of Ulysses, but that does not matter, the plot stands on broad mythic shoulders and is the stronger for it.

Myth has often been used as the basis of plot, not only in James Joyce's *Ulysses* but in Tolkien's *The Lord of the Rings*, Frank Herbert's *Dune* and its sequels and George Lucas's *Star Wars* series. What Joseph Campbell called the monomyth has been employed by writers who may not even be aware that they have fashioned their plots on the models of the House of Atreus, the Golden Fleece, Orpheus, Pygmalion and Galatea, Daedalus and Icarus, David and Goliath, David and Bathsheba, Samson and Delilah, Little Red Riding Hood and the wolf, Cinderella or the Passion of Christ.

Eugene O'Neill used the tragedy of the House of Atreus set against a Civil War backdrop in his *Mourning Becomes Electra*. In *The Stars in Their*

Courses, Harry Brown builds a western out of *The Iliad*, with water rights instead of Helen as the casus belli. The characters are identified with their mythic prototypes by the first letters of their names. Thus Achilles becomes Arch Eastmere; Priam, Percy Randall; Paris, Pax Randall; Hector, Hallock Randall, with Hallock identified, like Hector, as "breaker of horses."

How simple to convert the *Antigone* of Sophocles into a western. Thebes becomes a frontier fort, Creon the colonel. His lieutenant son is in love with the Sioux Princess Antigone, whose brother has been killed leading an attack of hostiles on the fort. His body is ordered by the colonel to lie unburied as a lesson to the hostiles, with death as the penalty for disobedience. But such an offense to Sioux holy laws cannot be tolerated by the Indian princess. She must bury the body against the edict of the colonel.

The plot can run its tragic course, or it can be given a happy ending by the arrival of a deus ex machina general, who countermands the colonel's cruel condemnation.

The symbols of mythology can stir the writer's creative juices. Books such as Joseph Campbell's *The Hero With a Thousand Faces*, Jung's *Man and His Symbols*, Jessie L. Weston's *From Ritual to Romance*, Robert Graves's *The White Goddess* and Lord Raglan's *The Hero* are powerful spurs to the imagination.

Lord Raglan's prescription for the hero follows:

1. The hero's mother is a holy virgin;
2. His father is a king, and
3. Often a near relative of his mother, but
4. The circumstances of his conception are unusual, and
5. He is also reputed to be the son of a god.
6. At birth an attempt is made on his life, usually by his father or his maternal grandmother, but
7. He is spirited away, and
8. Reared by foster parents in a far country.
9. We are told nothing of his childhood, but
10. On reaching manhood he returns or goes to his future kingdom.
11. After a victory over the king, and/or a giant, dragon, or wild beast,
12. He marries a princess, often the daughter of his predecessor, and (at about age thirty-four or thirty-five)

13. Becomes king.
14. For a time he reigns uneventfully, and
15. Prescribes laws, but
16. He later loses favor with the gods and/or his subjects and
17. Is driven from the throne or city, after which
18. He meets with a mysterious death,
19. Often at the top of a hill.
20. His children, if any, do not succeed him.
21. His body is not buried, but nevertheless
22. He has one or more holy tombs.

Oedipus ranks highest in terms of these requirements, with twenty-one out of twenty-two. Others, however, do very well: Jesus, David, Robin Hood, King Arthur, Billy the Kid, Butch Cassidy.

Classic novels also can be retreaded. How many fictional governesses have become Jane Eyre to their arrogant but eventually adoring masters? Daphne du Maurier was accused of plagiarism in her novel *Rebecca*, and she admitted that she had indeed borrowed the plot from Charlotte Brontë's classic.

In 1997 a new film of *Great Expectations* was released, based on the Dickens novel but set in the 1990s. A contemporary film was also made of Jane Austen's *Emma*. Diane Johnson's novel *Le Divorce* is admittedly related to Henry James's *The Portrait of a Lady*, and the protagonist is also named Isabel. Iris Murdoch's *An Unofficial Rose* is certainly a reworking of Jane Austen's *Mansfield Park*. *Gone With the Wind* owes a great debt to *Vanity Fair* (Becky Sharp/Scarlett O'Hara) and to *War and Peace*.

In her novel *Sarah Canary*, Karen Joy Fowler has borrowed the plot of *The Wizard of Oz*. Sarah is Dorothy; other characters fill in as the Scarecrow, the Cowardly Lion, the Tin Woodsman and the Wicked Witch. Fowler says, "I used that book quite consciously as a model to help me get from one end of my book to the other."

John Baldwin, who, in collaboration with an epidemiologist, John Marr, wrote a medical thriller titled *The Eleventh Plague* (after the biblical ten plagues of Egypt) that gained enormous publishing (and dollar advance) attention in 1998, patterned his novel on Robin Cook's thriller *Coma*, from which he sought to extract a formula. It was known that Cook had perused over one hundred medical thrillers to develop his plot and characters. Baldwin also studied the works of Tom Clancy and the noirish Hollywood films of the forties and fifties. Here follows the ten-step program Baldwin and Marr developed, as published in *The New York Times Magazine* in an article by Michael Maren:

1. The hero is an expert.
2. The villain is also an expert.
3. You must watch all the villany over the shoulder of the villain.
4. The hero has a team of experts in various fields behind him.
5. Two or more of the team must fall in love.
6. Two or more of the team must die.
7. The villain must turn his attention from his initial goal to the team.
8. The villain and the hero must live to do battle again in the sequel.
9. All deaths must proceed from the individual to the group: i.e., never say that the bomb exploded and 15,000 people were killed. Start with, "Jamie and Suzy were walking in the park with their grandmother when the earth opened up."
10. If you get bogged down, just kill somebody.

Michael Crichton's advice for thrillers is that there are certain "rules," for instance, that the storms, killer viruses or dinosaurs should become more dangerous as the novel progresses.

Borrowing

It has been said that *Oedipus Rex* is the original detective story, Oedipus both the detective and his quarry.

Louis L'Amour said that Sir Walter Scott's *Ivanhoe* was the first western. It has the first "walkdown" as a climax, although the walkdown is with broadswords rather than six-guns. In this fight in the 1997 TV production, Ivanhoe batters the Templar to death with his sword. This is not the same culmination as in the novel, however, where Bois-Guilbert has Ivanhoe at his mercy but cannot triumph because Ivanhoe has a moral ascendancy.

I used the idea of moral ascendancy as a theme in my western-historical novel *Warlock*. The hero-gunslinger, Clay Blaisedell, is always triumphant when he has "the right" on an opponent. When he does not, he, in effect, surrenders.

In the novel *Ivanhoe*, the Templar dies of heart failure from his conflicted emotions, leaving Ivanhoe his conqueror. In my novel *The Children of the Sun*, I borrowed this usage. My protagonist Dorantes must fight a duel with his old conquistador pal Caballo Botello, who saved his life in the retreat from Tenochtitlan on the "Sad Night." The fight is over the cruel treatment of the defeated indigenes, and Dorantes has the right on Caballo, who dies of heart failure as the duel begins. Thanks to Sir Walter Scott.

The following scene is from *Warlock*. Clay Blaisedell has killed his friend Morgan in a gun duel and brings his body inside a saloon, where a dramatic ceremony takes place:

> He pointed a finger at one of the barkeepers.
> "Bring me four candles over here." He turned slowly, in the dim room. "Take off your damned hats," he said.
> One of the bartenders scurried forward with four white candles. Blaisedell jammed one in the mouth of a whiskey bottle, lit it, and placed it beside Morgan's head. He took the bottle from the judge's table and lit a second candle, which he placed on the other side of Morgan's head. He handed the other two candles back to the barkeeper and indicated Morgan's feet.

Opera lovers will recall the scene in Puccini's *Tosca* where Floria Tosca has stabbed her molester, the villainous Scarpia, and performs a similar placing of candles beside his corpse.

The following is from *Homecoming*. The G.I. protagonist has participated in the liberation of the German prison camp at Mauthausen. In this scene he and a couple of soldiers surprise the evil camp commander, Colonel Haupt, in civilian clothes in the apartment of his mistress in the adjacent town. Haupt tells his captors that he lived for a time in the States and shares some memories with them, seeming a perfectly pleasant fellow:

> "There was a nice little bar where you could get a good lager,"

he went on. "Or a nice bottle of Gerolsteiner if you were inclined."

"Pat!" Bunker said, and I put my hand on the butt of the .45 when Haupt unbuttoned his jacket. He took the jacket off and laid it on the bed.

He made a gesture, as though requesting permission, and stepped to the big armoire against the wall. I drew the .45 as he opened the door of the armoire. He took from a hanger a Kraut uniform blouse and armed into it. It had a colonel's insignia on the collar, and the black lapels of the SS.

"I kept company with a pretty girl there," he went on. "Her father was an automobile dealer. She was very nice. Sometimes we would go for picnics."

He made the permission gesture again, and took a uniform cap from the shelf of the armoire and donned it. The cap had a high peak with the silver death's head of the SS adorning it. In the closet what looked like two lengths of stovepipe was a pair of black boots.

"She was a whore," he said suddenly harshly. Now he wore a colonel's cap and blouse, with the brown corduroy trousers and the striped tie. He had straightened so he was standing at attention, his shiny shoes set at right angles to each other.

I told him he was under arrest.

He shook his head. He had a little hair-line moustache like Errol Flynn's, which you didn't notice right away because of the darkness of his face.

"Ah, no," he said. His voice had become deeper, that harsh Teutonic bark. "I will only surrender to a person of proper rank," he said. "I will not surrender to a sergeant."

"Yes, you will," I said.

This scene pays tribute to Bertolt Brecht's play *The Life of Galileo*. There the Pope is being dressed in his ceremonial robes. Ungarbed he is a regular person, liberal, almost a "pleasant fellow," but as he dons the stiff, formal and emblematic robes, he turns into the pontiff. Here, Haupt, in his blouse and cap, changes into a Nazi officer and speaks and acts accordingly.

Compulsion

"Give him a compulsion and let him go," is Ray Bradbury's advice. Compulsions and ambitions fuel the plot. The ambitious heroes of nineteenth-century novels such as Stendhal's Julian Sorel, the heroes of Balzac, even Emma Bovary were known as "desiring machines."

My novel *Corpus of Joe Bailey*, which concerns a young man growing up in San Diego during the Depression and World War II, has a so-called bitch heroine, a desiring machine. These ladies, such as Lady Brett in *The Sun Also Rises*, Caddy in *The Sound and the Fury*, Sally Bowles of *The Berlin Stories* and *I Am a Camera*, as well as the heroines of many novels by Aldous Huxley and Evelyn Waugh, were common in the twenties. The heroines were doomed beautiful bad girls. My own such a one was named Constance Robinson.

The book was published in 1953, was a best-seller, was condemned from the pulpit in San Diego and banned in England and Australia. Now it seems rather mild, but it was satisfyingly shocking in its time.

Many years later I was invited back to San Diego by the San Diego Historical Society for a discussion of my old novel, which I discovered was still renowned among my generation there. I thought these gray-haired men were interested in my hero, Joe Bailey, because their life experiences had been similar to his. Not at all. Like many readers, they tended to think that fictional characters were based on real ones, and they were interested in Con Robinson. On what San Diego girl of the forties was she modelled? They suspected that there was a hot number that I had had access to and they had not.

I couldn't bear to tell them that Con Robinson was based on Emma Bovary.

Plots of Quest, Plots of Mystery

A quest is Oliver Twist's search for his parents; a mystery, the puzzle of who they are. Many contemporary novels are based on a search for identity.

Who am I? A psychological mystery would be a Freudian inquiry into how the dysfunctional protagonist got that way.

An important aspect of the mystery novel is the Oedipal Plot. This is not an inquiry into Oedipus's relationship with his mother, but into his former life. In the Oedipal Plot a messenger arrives from the past with information that drastically affects the present, or the past is searched for such information. Many mystery novels are constructed on this base.

High Life/Low Life

Oedipus, the king, is connected with the past by a shepherd (low life), whose task it was to expose the infant Oedipus on the mountain (that is, dispose of him). Thus the guilt that has brought the plague on Thebes is uncovered by a conjunction of high life and low life. Shakespeare of course employed low-life characters (speaking in prose) along with his nobles and kings (who converse in iambic pentameter). Dickens's plots are often high life–low life; for instance, in *Bleak House*, the puzzle of relationships is solved when the essential vertical connection is made. John Fowles's *The French Lieutenant's Woman* is constructed with a double plot, including high-life and low-life characters. Raymond Chandler's mysteries use that motif, with the murders solved by a final connection, for instance, the discovery that the high-society Mrs. Grayle of *Farewell, My Lovely* was at one time the low-society stripper Velma.

Sara Paretsky in her mystery novel *Blood Shot* uses this formula. The detective, V.I. Warshawski, is a hard-boiled Chicago lady private eye. The area of her expertise is Chicago politics, from the lowest level to the highest. The connection of the low life to the high constitutes the solution of the central mystery.

Warshawski returns to her native south Chicago for a reunion of a high school girl's basketball team. There she receives two commissions, one from a young woman who was her admirer as a girl—to search for the young woman's lost father. The other is to discover why the local alderman has come out against a project that would seem of great benefit to South Chicago.

The former is the low-life plot; the latter takes Warshawski into upper-level Chicago politics. Early in the novel the reader may be able to figure out that the alderman is the disappeared father, but there is plenty of suspense and surprise along the way, including an Oedipal Plot—a reeking injustice of long ago that must be solved and brought to bear on the present.

In historical novels the writer needs be concerned with his low-life plot as well as the high one, for as Max Byrd has written, "Historical fiction gives the history of a tribe, and the whole tribe has to be represented," the shepherd as well as Oedipus, Theristes as well as Achilles, Sally Hemings as well as Thomas Jefferson.

Sir Walter Scott's protagonists are usually neutral in their politics, for the author is thus able to bring the reader with them into the opposing camps. In *Ivanhoe*, the eponymous character is an aristocratic adherent of compromise between the Saxons and their Norman conquerors. Richard Coeur de Lion is also such a (Norman) moderate. Ivanhoe's father, however, is an uncompromising Saxon. The Saxon serfs Gurth and Wamba must be won to moderate stance along with their betters. Thus there is the interaction between "above" and "below," *Upstairs, Downstairs*, nobility and commoners, low life and high life, that constitutes the span of the populace at that period.

Plot Devices

The MacGuffin

The object of a quest is often a "MacGuffin," a term used in fiction and film for the searched-for object. In Louis B. Jones's *California's Over*, the box containing the poet-father's ashes is actually labelled "MacGuffin," as though that is the name of the undertakers who cremated the body, rather than the author's sly joke. The Maltese falcon in the film and the novel of that name is just such an object. So is the safe-deposit key both the good guys and the bad guys are trying to locate, so is the vial of superstrength bubonic plague imported from Iraq that will infect the nation if it is not found and destroyed, so is the murdered ambassador's diary in my novel *A Game for Eagles*, the stash of opium in Robert Stone's *Dog Soldiers*, Wilkie Collins's great diamond the Moonstone, the baseball that Bobby

Thomson hit for a home run that won the pennant for the the New York Giants over the Brooklyn Dodgers in Don DeLillo's novel *Underworld*. So is Moby Dick, so is the Holy Grail in the Arthurian legends.

The Boo Radley Mechanism

Another serviceable plot device might be called the Boo Radley Mechanism. In *To Kill a Mockingbird*, Boo Radley is the hermit who lives near the protagonist, Scout, and never shows himself, until he appears opportunely at the end of the novel to kill the crazy cracker who is determined to murder Scout for revenge on her lawyer father. In David Hunt's *The Magician's Tale*, a hermit hippy lives concealed in the park opposite the heroine's apartment house and conveniently sallies out to save her from the attack of the bad guys.

Angels have also been used for this purpose.

Such a device must be prepared for early on, and not simply show up as needed, like the Marines, the cavalry or The Black Watch with bagpipes blaring. In Greek drama, the term *deus ex machina*, "the god from a machine," describes a device used to save the day when the author could not plot his characters reasonably out of trouble. Hercules, riding some stage machinery, swoops down to carry the endangered one off to Olympus.

The Gun on the Wall

In P.D. James's novel *A Certain Justice*, early on there is a scene of detective Adam Dalgliesh's two young assistants, Kate Miskin and Piers Tarrant, qualifying with automatic weapons at a police range. This is a contract with the reader that guns will play their part in the novel, and indeed, at the climax, Piers shoots dead the murderer who is holding the young girl captive.

Anton Chekhov as a playwright made the famous statement that if you show a gun hanging on the wall in act one, you had better discharge the weapon in act three. The reverse is also true. If you discharge a weapon in act three, you had better have shown it beforehand. So with the machine (deus ex) that swoops down with Hercules aboard to carry off the distressed heroine. The author had better show that machine earlier, ruminating in its stall ready for action.

In Janet Fitch's fine novel *White Oleander*, there is an episode in which the protagonist, walking along a familiar street, is attacked by two dogs, who bite her severely about the face. In this case the discharged gun has never been hung on the wall. The dogs have not been shown previously as being a theatening presence, in fact they have never been previously shown at all, nor is there any particular reason for them to attack the girl on this day. Of course this kind of accident happens frequently in life, but in this case, without gun-on-the-wall preparation, it is not successfully fictionalized.

In *The Prince of Tides*, however, Pat Conroy carefully prepares for a highly improbable scene where a tiger kills a gang of rapists. It was a time when gasoline advertising celebrated a "tiger in your tank" and the father of the protagonist's family owns a gas station. He purchases a threadbare tiger to reinforce the gasoline advertising, and the tiger becomes something of a household pet. When the evildoers infest the household to rape the mother and the sister, the tiger, which has by now been well established, kills them.

Earthquakes shake Los Angeles fairly often, and certainly it is common for newspaper headlines to announce their destructions. But in fiction that action must be foreshadowed, hung on the wall so to speak, with a series of smaller earthquakes leading up to the big one, or the cats and dogs going crazy and howling with foreknowledge.

Boundaries

Henry James sets this problem:

> Really, universally, relations stop nowhere, and the exquisite problem of the artist is eternally but to draw, by a geometry of his own, the circle within which they shall *happily* appear to do so.

The circle is a Grand Hotel, within which all the characters are ensconced; the English country house, fenced off from the great world, in which the murder suspects are housed. Traditionally, by the above rules of guns on the wall, the actual murderer has been one of those so confined within James's circle. But mystery story writers such as Patricia Cornwell and Caleb Carr, who specialize in serial killers, have complicated their problems. Their killers reside outside the parameters, in the country, or world at large, and the trick for the authors is to find the means of bringing those characters inside for recognition and justice.

Plot Progression

The plot opens with a situation, a character in some kind of predicament; relationships, compulsions and oppositions are established. The characters are in conflict with each other or with some outside force (the army, the police, school, parents, society, tradition, religion). The conflicts intensify in what is called the complication, to the crisis, followed by the resolution.

Situation, complication and resolution can also be seen as a three-act structure. Hemingway's *The Sun Also Rises* is actually divided into Books One, Two and Three like Acts. Book One sets up the situation and the relationships. Book Two brings the characters to Pamplona for the fiesta and complicates the relationships. Book Three resolves the problems with character change.

In the three-act structure on stage, the first- and second-act curtains mark major reversals or recognitions. The first-act curtain denotes the end of the movement establishing characters and situation, galvanizing or reversing it. The second-act curtain ends the movement of complication and confrontation, in preparation for the final movement of resolution. In opera the second act is often climaxed by an "avalanche curtain," which crashes down on the sustained high C of the tenor's great aria at the opera's most dramatic moment.

Powerful fiction has a line of compulsion as strong as a hawser running from beginning to end. The reader is compelled because the characters are compelled. The hawser is composed of strands, one in a short story, many in a complicated, many-generational novel. Each character is provided with a through-line, what he wants overall, and what he wants in a particular scene or moment. Shorter strands of tension run shorter distances of situation and resolution, from page 3 to page 5, from page 4 to page 20, from page 11 to page 250. The hawser is woven of these lines of tension so that the reader is not only provided with a main plotline but with sufficient other lines of suspense or tension to rivet interest. If there is only a long line of tension with insufficient short lines, the reader may skip to the end to see how the plot turns out; if there are short lines without long lines, the reader will quit reading when his short-term curiosity is satisfied.

In Charles Portis's *Gringos*, the narrator is threatened by an evil band of hippies called the Jumping Jacks. He gets the drop on them with his shotgun, and in his rage tears the electric cables out of their car and breaks the windshield and windows. Here is a contract, then, author to reader, that the Jumping Jacks will reappear, probably with the advantage next time. This line of suspense is kept alive by mentioning signs of their whereabouts from time to time as the plot progresses.

The Ticking Clock

Sometimes the Ticking Clock is called the Time Crunch; for example, if Ben hasn't climbed Mount Diablo by ten o'clock this morning the neo-Nazi skinheads will crucify his wife in their barbaric rites.

In *Cat on a Hot Tin Roof,* if Maggie doesn't produce an heir before Big Daddy dies, the plantation will fall into the hands of the No-neck Monsters.

Notice the attention to time paid by P.D. James in *Original Sin.*

Chapter one:

> For a temporary shorthand-typist to be present at the discovery of a corpse on the *first day* of a new assignment, if not unique, is sufficiently rare to prevent its being regarded as an occupational hazard. Certainly Mandy Price, aged nineteen years two months, and the acknowledged star of Mrs. Crealey's Nonesuch Secretarial Agency, set out on the morning of *Tuesday 14 September. . . .* (Emphasis added.)

Chapter four:

> *Ten days after Sonia Clements' suicide and exactly three weeks* before the first of the Innocent House murders, Adam Dalgliesh . . . (Emphasis added.)

Chapter ten:

> *Mandy's first four weeks* at Innocent House . . . (Emphasis added.)

Chapter fifty-two:

> Velma Pitt-Cowley, Mrs. Carling's literary agent, had agreed *to be at the flat at 11:30 and arrived six minutes late.* . . . (Emphasis added.)

Most of this time sticklerism is of no consequence except for the ticking clock's demands, although often James uses it very cleverly, as in chapter four's "exactly three weeks before the first of the Innocent House murders," where readers are forewarned of murders to come.

Again it becomes a useful suspense device in James's *A Certain Justice.* On page 3:

> When, on the afternoon of Wednesday, 11 September, Venetia Aldridge stood up to cross-examine the prosecution's chief witness in the case of *Regina v. Ashe, she had four weeks, four hours and fifty minutes left of life.* (Emphasis added.)

And again on page 36:

> *She had less than four weeks left of life.* (Emphasis added.)

Recognitions and Revelations

Fiction progresses on recognitions and revelations like rolling on casters, or to change the figure, like doses of vitamins. In *Blood Shot*, it is both a recognition and a revelation when the alderman is revealed as the long lost father. It is a terrible recognition for Oedipus to realize his wife is his mother. Oedipus limps because his ankles were pierced when he was abandoned on the mountain, a recognition. Ulysses is recognized by his scarred foot by the servant who bathes him. The former concentration camp inmate is recognized by the camp number tattooed inside her wrist, the Armenian sex slave by her Turkish owner's name tattooed on her neck. In *The Portrait of a Lady*, Isabel Archer realizes her husband's long and close acquaintance with Madame Merle on viewing them in postures of easy intimacy, a revelation. In *The Ambassadors*, Lambert Strether has a revelation of Chad and Madame de Vionnet's relationship when he sees them boating on the river.

Authorial promises can also be made that create suspense in revelations of conduct or problems to come. They become a kind of contract with the reader. When it is revealed that the snake bite kit has disappeared from the glove compartment of the pickup truck, we have an inkling that that kit may be needed in pages to come.

Endings

In a mystery novel the solution, presented by the detective, is a surprise, but, on reflection, totally logical and prepared for. If the author were to produce a ragged stranger who has never appeared in the story before as the culprit, he would get angry faxes from his readers. The ending should be surprising but inevitable. There has been change, and the change is shown or proven.

In Henry James's *The Wings of the Dove*, Merton Densher and Kate Croy are in love but Densher is too poor to marry a girl with great expectations. Enter Milly Theale, an heiress who is dying. The two lovers contrive for Milly to fall in love with Densher. They will marry, Milly will die, and her fortune will enable Densher and Kate Croy to marry. When Milly dies it is discovered that she knew all about the plot, but she forgives the plotters and has left Densher a fortune. The secret love of Densher and Kate Croy is poisoned by Milly's goodness. Both of them have changed. Kate's final statement is, "We will never again be as we were!"

Square One With Change

> We shall not cease from exploration
> And the end of all our exploring
> Will be to arrive where we started

And know the place for the first time

—T.S. Eliot, "Little Gidding"

My novel *Apaches* begins with the following scene. Lieutenant Cutler of the U.S. Cavalry is in charge of a detail of Apache scouts in 1880s New Mexico:

> Following his Apache trackers up the swale through jumbles of paddle cactus and ocotillo whips, Cutler saw them gathered on the ridge, pointing, laughing: six of them, dirty brown legs under their filthy shirts astride brown ponies, long black hair in turbans. Nochte pumped his carbine up and down twice in a signal.
>
> Cutler spurred on up the slope, so tired from two weeks of chasing hostiles he could hardly dig his heels in, and Blackie too tired to respond. Tazzi shouted down to him in the Indian way, as though white men were deaf, "Ho, look, white-eye loco!"
>
> Down the far swale were two prospectors and their mules, ragged and dusty, with sweat-dark hats pulled low on their faces. One sat on the ground with his pick across his legs and rifle cradled in his arms, staring down at it as though afraid to look up at the cat-calling Apaches on the ridge. The other scrambled up a red-earth cutbank, not quite gaining the top, keeping his feet with difficulty. He took another run and failed again, and he too never looked up at the ridge.

The prospectors are insane with fear, for torture and murder is what they can expect if captured by the Apaches of that time.

A similar scene is employed at the end. Years have passed, the railroad has come, Apacheria has been tamed, Cutler is bidding his scouts farewell on a knoll from which the railroad tracks are visible. A handcar comes along it, pumped by two men (as there were two prospectors earlier). These wave a friendly hand at Cutler and the Apache scouts as they pass by. Times have changed.

A similar disposition is employed in *Madame Bovary*. The reader first meets Emma in her father's farmhouse, where Charles Bovary comes to call. She offers him a glass of liquor and takes one herself. Tongue protruding, she licks drop by drop the bottom of her glass. At the end of the novel we see her lying dead of poison, her tongue, blackened with arsenic, protruding.

A change on this is rung in the motion picture *Elizabeth*, which begins with the heads of three protestant martyrs being shaved for their execution and ends with Elizabeth herself taking on the aspect of the virgin queen by shearing off her own beautiful hair.

The Rights of Characters

Often a novelist plots with a given ending in mind. Plotting is sometimes best accomplished backward, moving from the resolution back to the climax then to the framing of the original situation. But the plotter, when it comes to the writing, had better listen to the complaints and suggestions of the characters as they acquire a life and mind of their own. John Fowles had this to say about the writing of *The French Lieutenant's Woman*:

> I was stuck this morning to find a good answer from Sarah in the climax of a scene. Characters sometimes reject all possibilities one offers. They say, in effect: I would never say or do a thing like that. But they don't say what they would say; and one has to proceed negatively, by a very tedious coaxing kind of trial and error.

Joyce Carol Oates describes this same phenomenon:

> My characters really dictate themselves to me. I can not force them into situations they haven't themselves willed.

Nabokov, however, is reported to have said, "My characters cringe when I come near them."

I am working on a historical mystery novel that I've called *The Death of Kings* because it is arranged around the death of King Kalakaua of the Kingdom of Hawaii in San Francisco in 1891. A character known as the Monarch of the California Poets (death of *kings*) was to be the villain, and when his niece discovers that he has lied to her about her paternity, she murders him. The ending had her confined in an asylum for the criminally insane. This character, Haunani, doesn't want anything to do with the fate I had planned for her. She doesn't want to murder her uncle, and she doesn't want to go crazy. I'm listening to her.

First Aid for Plots

1. Remember that plot is character in predicament.
2. The protagonist should be the initiator of the action rather than the victim of it, active rather than passive.
3. Is there use for a Ticking Clock?
4. Give the protagonist a compulsion. Consider the compulsions in *The Wizard of Oz*: Dorothy wants to get home to Kansas, the Tin Woodsman wants a heart, the Scarecrow a brain, the Wicked Witch the ruby slipper.
5. Consider unities and contractual obligations. If the novel begins in Santa Ana, California, maybe it should end in Santa Ana. If Ralph appears on page 10, maybe he should reappear before the end of the novel. If there is a bear trap hung on the wall in the first chapter, maybe it should be actuated in the last.
6. What is at stake?
7. Is the ending inevitable yet surprising?

PART II

Forms of
Fiction

CHAPTER 9

The Short Story

... something glimpsed from the corner of the eye, in passing.

—V.S. PRITCHETT

The short story writer Edith Templeton says of her stories, in a piece in *The New Yorker*, that they are "outside facts painted with subjective feelings." This may be as good a definition of the contemporary short story as anything.

The definition has become increasingly comprehensive. Is there some point of length where a short story becomes a minute story? Another where a short story becomes a novella or novelette? Is there a requirement for character change? "From that day forth everything was as it were changed, and appeared in a different light to him" (Gogol). Not anymore. Is the establishment of a mood or a character sufficient? If it satisfies.

There is no such thing as an essential form. In a way the writer invents a new form with each attempt, with all the chances for triumph or disaster.

Raymond Carver kept a card taped above his desk on which he had printed in block letters "Tell the story."

He had another three-by-five with a fragment of a sentence from Chekhov: ". . . and suddenly everything became clear to him."

Flannery O'Connor points out that stories are full of material stuff. Stories do not come out of perceptions of spirit or thoughts but of the perceptions of *things*. These are the outside facts of which Edith Templeton speaks. The writer must take these outside facts, these *things,* and endow them with subjective feelings.

Regard the mileage John O'Hara obtains from the outside facts in the first paragraph of his story "Appearances" from *The Cape Cod Lighter*:

> Howard Ambrie stopped the car at the porte cochere to let his wife out, then proceeded to the garage. The MG was already there, the left-hand door was open, and the overhead lamp was burning, indicating that their daughter was home. Ambrie put the sedan in its customary place, snapped out the light, rang down the door, and walked slowly toward the house. He stopped midway and looked at the sky. The moon was high and plain, the stars were abundant.

What has the author told us in these few lines? That Ambrie and his wife are well enough off to live in a house with a porte cochere, and to be able to indulge their daughter with a fancy little MG (this is a car that is no longer manufactured but was very popular in the forties and fifties when it gave its owners a kind of raffish, go-to-hell character). Not only that, but the daughter has piled out of her car in a hurry, leaving the left-hand door open and the overhead light on. We are not told that the father is irritated or troubled by this, but thought is implied in his stopping midway to the house to gaze up at the moon.

Eudora Welty felt that plot made the short story heavy and flat. She equated plot with the novel, a form with which she was uncomfortable, and she considered plot, no matter how intriguing, to be always superficial. She considered her own stories as pitting situation against character. "Complete revealing" of the secrets of human life, she believed to be the province of the short story.

In a good story, the characters are revealed through the action and the action is controlled through the characters. The challenge of the short story writer is to make the action describe or reveal as many of the secrets of existence as possible. The writer does this through the employment of the senses, and detail. Fiction is not a matter of saying things; it is a matter of showing things—again those outside facts. It is possible to write about commonplace facts, things—a ring, a sofa, a bed, curtains, a teapot—with much more power than of the flourishing of grand abstract ideas.

The short story must work on a much swifter assemblage than the novel. More has to be accomplished in less space; the details, the things, have to carry more weight, often becoming symbolic in their action within the story, which is to say that the details work on the literal level of the story, but in depth as well as on the surface, increasing the impact and the meaning.

Carver speaks of turning life's stories into short fiction:

> You have to be immensely daring, very skilled and imaginative and willing to tell everything on yourself. . . .
>
> And the secrets revealed had better be the real ones, and not the less demanding defenses and rationalizations against those secrets.

"Of course all writing is based on personal experience," Margaret Atwood says. "But personal experience is experience—wherever it comes from—that you identify with, *imagine* if you like, so that it becomes personal to you."

My own short stories that hold up in my own estimation stem from some concrete object, from a terrible thorn from the Holy Land, from a high, dangerous concrete retaining wall, from a country girl whore lynched (her body left hanging over a canyon as a warning) for receiving stolen calves in return for tricks, from the shooting of a tomcat.

The concrete objects retain the power that incited the story in the first place.

Serendipity

When writing is "in the zone," its magnetism draws attributes to it: an item in the paper that is just what was needed, an article perused for no reason, a story told on the telephone, a postcard from an old friend recalling a pertinent incident. All may instantly become a part of the fabric.

Carver recalls being in the middle of a story when the telephone rang. An African-American voice asked for someone named Nelson. Carver found himself including a character named Nelson in his story, a somewhat sinister black man. The story took a new tack, which was the right tack.

Margaret Atwood says this about serendipity:

> Art happens. It happens when you have the craft and the vocation and are waiting for something else, something extra, or

maybe not waiting; in any case it happens. It's the extra rabbit coming out of the hat, the one you didn't put there.

Flannery O'Connor comments on why stories work:

> I often ask myself what makes a story work, and what makes it hold up as a story, and I have decided that it is probably some action, some gesture of a character that is unlike any other in the story, one which indicates where the real heart of the story lies. This would have to be an action or gesture which was both totally right and totally unexpected. . . .

It would be Margaret Atwood's rabbit out of the hat that had not been put there.

Epiphany

A literary epiphany, as we have seen, is a kind of numinous superrevelation.

In the fifties short story writers strained every fiber of memory and imagination to come up with epiphanies with which to end their stories. This era is, fortunately, past. Stories are no longer dependent upon epiphanies.

One of the three-by-five cards that Carver contemplated mounting on the wall over his desk read "No tricks."

Beginner's Stories

Here follow two short stories of my own. They were written when I was a beginning writer. They were not published in *The New Yorker*, but they were published, which was my intention and my hope. They both derived from concrete objects, both from felt emotions—from outside facts and subjective feelings. Flannery O'Connor wrote that:

> The fact is that anybody who has survived his childhood has enough information about life to last him the rest of his days.

These are stories of childhood survivals. "The Crown" is based on a situation and a person that were deeply meaningful to me, "The Retaining

Wall," on a hazardous and symbolic place. In the former story a lot of things were done right, in the latter some basic things went wrong.

These are stories from the store of fictional material every writer can call up from youthful experience.

THE CROWN

He had been awake for some time when he heard his mother calling him. He crossed his arms over his stomach and pressed down hard. He was really sick today, all right. They wouldn't make him go to school if he was really sick. He wouldn't have to see her sitting there with her nose bleeding now till after Easter vacation, and maybe after Easter his father would get him transferred to Horace Mann Grammar School so that he would never have to see her again at all.

"Mom, I'm sick!" he called back. "I'm pretty sick to my stomach this morning."

But he knew it wasn't going to work. He could hear them talking downstairs, his sister's voice louder than his mother's or father's. He heard his father's heavy steps on the living room rug. Quickly he sat up and swung his legs over the edge of the bed, rubbing his stomach and practicing making faces. The sun came in across the bed and brightened the backs of the Oz books on the bottom shelf of his bookcase. He heard his father coming up the stairs.

Then his father was standing in the doorway; moving his head a little he could see the shining brown shoes, the right one slightly advanced. "Get moving, kid," his father said. "I told you we weren't going through this again. What's the matter with you, anyway?"

"I don't feel good." He sucked his breath in through his teeth and massaged his stomach. His father just stood there watching him, jingling the change in his pocket. He rose and began to take off his pajamas. He knew it wasn't going to do any good to argue, or cry. But he felt like crying.

"I've got the pictures all ready for you to take, dear!" his mother called from downstairs.

He got a clean pair of BVDs from his top drawer, sidled out the door past his father and went into the bathroom. He felt a little better, remembering the pictures. After lunch today, the last day before Easter vacation, everyone in

Miss Erwin's class was to give a three-minute talk. He was going to tell about the Olympic Games. He was the only one in the fifth grade who had seen the Olympic Games at Los Angeles last summer, and he was going to show the pictures his father had taken. Miss Erwin had said it should be very interesting. He tried to think about showing the pictures, instead of about Dorothy Mason.

It didn't do any good. Today would be just like all the other days. She would not be in her seat when the bell rang and there would be the minutes of hope that she would not come today. But then there would be the sound of her footsteps, faint at first, then louder, unmistakable, and next to him Dick Stafford would start making faces, pinching his nose between his fingers and crossing his eyes. He wished Dick would not do it. It was not enough. It was not even right.

She had come into the fifth grade a few days after the beginning of the term. He had heard in the hall the brisk clatter of Mr. Proctor's steps and with it the slow, dragging sound that, although he did not know it then, meant that Dorothy Mason was coming.

Miss Erwin had turned quickly from the blackboard, picked up her ruler and tapped on her desk with it. She said, "There will be a little lame girl coming into the class this morning. I know you will all be very courteous to her."

He looked as the door opened. Behind him, Mary Sebastian's pigtails swung across her back. After the first glance at Dorothy Mason, he looked away, staring down at his desk, then at the spelling lesson on the board, then out the window where the sun was bright on the bare ground. The arches of the opposite wing made thick, curved shadows. At the end of the patio the bicycles were parked and he concentrated on trying to make out his own among the others there.

Miss Erwin stepped forward to show Dorothy Mason her seat, which was in the second row between Betty Andrews and Iris Black. The shuffling sound came down the aisle. He watched her as she passed. She was very small. She walked jerkily with her knees bent and stiff, as though she could only move her legs at the hips. Her elbows were pressed against her sides and her narrow, dangling hands looked like flippers. Her dress was yellow, her hair was a faded yellow, and her smiling face was chalky white.

Miss Erwin and Mr. Proctor helped her to her seat and then went out into the hall together. No one spoke or even moved. He stared straight ahead of him at the words written on the blackboard in Miss Erwin's round, neat writing. There were five columns of them, and on the upper left corner of the board there was an irregular blob of sunlight. Just when he began to feel like he was under water holding his breath and couldn't hold it much longer, Miss Erwin came back in.

"This is the spelling lesson," Miss Erwin said to Dorothy Mason, smiling and pointing to the words on the blackboard. "We are copying the words now and tomorrow we'll have a spelling test." Dorothy Mason nodded. There was a black and white bow at the side of her faded hair. He watched her writing the words, holding the pencil like a dagger. He had finished copying the lesson long before, and he knew everyone else had too. The only sound was the slow scratching of Dorothy Mason's pencil. His own hand began to feel wet with sweat, and it ached as he gripped his own pencil, wishing her to hurry.

Miss Erwin was holding the ruler, smiling a funny smile that looked as though her lips were stuck to her teeth. She was tall and she always wore a white blouse and a black skirt, which would be smudged with chalk by the end of first period. She was the prettiest teacher he had ever had, and she made everything interesting and real. Sixth period she always told the class a story and her stories were even better than those his mother told. They were about people like George Washington, or Lincoln, or Edison; sometimes they were about Jesus, and those stories always made him feel the way his book of Christmas stories did, a little sad but happy at the same time and as though Jesus would have been a *very* nice man to know—as nice perhaps as Miss Erwin who almost always took someone's side against Mr. Proctor or the teacher in charge of the cafeteria and who would lend them lunch money if they lost theirs and who helped them after school if they were failing in anything. He wondered what Miss Erwin was going to do about Dorothy Mason.

Only a few days later Dorothy Mason had had the first nose bleed. It was during sixth period and Miss Erwin was telling a story about a boy named Milo who picked up a calf every day when he was little, so that as he grew and the calf grew, he could still pick it up. When she had finished,

Bill Waters had his hand up. "My father says you shouldn't ever try to pick up anything heavy like that," he said. "He says you'll hurt yourself."

"But you see, Bill," Miss Erwin said, "Milo picked up the calf every single day, and each day it was only just a little heavier."

He raised his hand and waved it. When Miss Erwin called on him, he said, "At the Olympic Games we saw a guy pick up a big weight like that. Big old pieces of iron on the ends of this bar. He lifted it way up. I guess it must've been almost as heavy as this bull, wasn't it, Miss Erwin?" Miss Erwin smiled, but it was the smile with her lips stuck against her teeth: and he saw then that Dorothy Mason had her hand up: her white, thin arm was raised, with the elbow bent and then the wrist bent so her hand pointed back at herself. She looked like she was shading her eyes from the sun. "Yes, Dorothy?" Miss Erwin said.

And Dorothy Mason said, "The heaviest weight was the cross Our Saviour carried." Her voice was high and quavering, with a kind of rusty catch to it, and as she spoke his heart began to beat faster. He felt as he had once when he had said a bad word in front of his mother, or as if he had been caught in some terrible lie. He looked down at his desk, seeing, out of the corners of his eyes, Dick Stafford staring down too, and on the other side of Dick, Elizabeth Homes peeling the paint off her pencil and frowning fiercely.

"And He had to carry it all the way up that terrible hill," Dorothy Mason went on. "He had to carry that terrible cross all the way up that hill after they had beaten Him and spit on Him and crowned Him with thorns, and at the top . . ."

He tried not to listen. He shut his eyes and made himself try not to listen, as though by pressing his eyes tight shut he was shutting his ears too. But he heard her still, and hearing her was like the picture of Jesus on the cross at his Grandmother Searle's house that had frightened him and, when he had grown older, had embarrassed him and made him feel ashamed: the caved-in stomach and the bleeding hands and feet, the bleeding hole in His side, the gaunt, suffering face and the trickles of blood on His cheeks from the thorns.

"All right, Dorothy," he heard Miss Erwin say. Feet scuffled behind him. But Dorothy Mason didn't stop and Miss Erwin said, "That's enough now

Dorothy. We . . ." She sounded very courteous and he shook his head violently, looking up as the *rusty,* terrible voice continued. Miss Erwin's face was as white as Dorothy Mason's. Her mouth opened and closed twice, like a fish's mouth, and then she cried, "Did you *hear* me? I said that's *enough!*" And Dorothy Mason stopped.

He could look at her then, and he knew that *everyone* was looking at her, for Miss Erwin had never raised her voice like that before. She was staring back at Miss Erwin, and finally he saw her smile. It was not an embarrassed smile, it was forgiving. When Miss Erwin told the class to study the geography lesson for a test tomorrow, he could hardly understand what she was saying.

At that moment he saw Dorothy Mason put one of her thin hands to her nose. Then she raised her hand and when she turned toward Miss Erwin he could see the blood. It came in a stream out of her nose, the stream parting over her chin, meeting again below it and dripping down the front of her dress. The blood was vivid red on her white face. He heard Dick suck in his breath. Miss Erwin seemed frozen, Room 8 a place he had never been before. And then Miss Erwin's hoarse voice told Warren Kleinschmidt to run for the nurse.

Dorothy Mason had a nose bleed in class almost every week after that, but after the first day a kind of system developed, like a fire drill. Iris Black and Phyllis Henderson traded seats, and as soon as Phyllis or Betty Andrews saw that the bleeding had begun, they would jump up and get towels and a basin of water from the lavatory. One of them would hold a wet towel to the back of Dorothy Mason's neck while the other wiped the blood from her face. Dorothy Mason would sit up very straight, her elbows propped on the edge of the desk and her long thin hands pointing back at her chest, with the blood coming down over her mouth and being mopped away.

He began to hate school. He dreaded meeting Dorothy Mason in the hall. She would smile and he and whoever was with him would have to smile back and then pretend they were talking about something important as they walked on. Or, if he was alone, he would have to pretend he was in a hurry, looking for someone he had to find right away. He dreaded class because when Miss Erwin asked a question, Dorothy Mason's hand almost always went up first, and the hand was crippled, the hand crooked, and it seemed somehow to be his fault. Miss Erwin would not notice the hand, looking instead for someone else to call on, but many times, and more and more often, there would be no other hand, and the strained smile would come to Miss Erwin's face and she would have to turn and say, "Dorothy?" And Dorothy Mason would answer in her thin, rusty voice.

He was afraid to talk about her with anyone. She was never mentioned, except in the look Dick Stafford gave him each morning when they heard the dragging foot steps. He had never even told his mother and father about her when they asked why he didn't like school anymore. But he hated her for making him feel that in some queer way he was to blame. Each morning when his mother called, each breakfast when his father got mad at him for saying he was sick, each time Cathy made fun of him for trying to get out of going to school, each time he saw Dorothy Mason or heard her shuffling feet in the hallway, or even thought of her, he wished she would die.

Now as he hurried down the hall he glanced at the bulletin board across from the third graders' room. It was covered with the third graders' Easter pictures: crayon drawings of rabbits and eggs with designs on them and little yellow chicks, grouped in various ways. Each one had a crookedly printed name at the lower right hand corner. The buzzer rang just as he opened the door to Room 8. Miss Erwin was passing out paper for a history test and Dorothy Mason was already in her seat. She was wearing the black and white bow and the yellow dress she had worn her first day in the class. Beside her desk was a black box almost a foot square. He stared at it as he placed the shoe box of pictures of the Olympic Games on his own desk and sat down. Dick Stafford was absent.

Fourth period the talks began. Johnny Anderson told about the Grand Canyon. Iris Black told about her guinea pigs. He didn't listen to them, staring at the black box beside Dorothy Mason's desk. When Dorothy Mason's turn came Betty helped her to the table that faced the class and Warren Kleinschmidt carried the black box up for her. She was going to talk on the Holy Land, she said, and she had some pictures to show. She held up each photograph, but they were too small for him to see. There were pictures of the mount where Jesus had given a sermon and of a place called Golgotha, and a great many were of buildings in Jerusalem. She handed each picture to Miss Erwin, who looked at it briefly before starting it around the class.

Finally there were no more pictures and Dorothy Mason took from the box what looked like a circle of very large barbed wire. She held it in her hands, which were bent awkwardly back so that it almost touched her chest. Her voice changed. It became louder, sing-song, and at first he could not make out what she was talking about.

"He was taken to the judgment hall," he heard her say. "And there Pilate said unto Him, 'Art thou the king of the Jews?' And Our Saviour said, 'To this end was I born, and for this cause came I into the world. . . .' "

He couldn't look at her any more. He couldn't make himself look at her. He could only stare down at the box containing the pictures of the Olympic Games, or up at Miss Erwin who was standing stiffly to one side with her face very white and chalk marks on the hips of her skirt and her eyes fixed on the spiked ring Dorothy Mason held. He stared at her pleadingly, as Dorothy Mason's voice seemed to rise higher at every word: "And Pilate said, 'But ye have a custom that I should release to you one at the Passover. Will you that I release unto you the king of the Jews?' Then they all cried again, 'Not this man, but Barabbas!' And Barabbas was a robber!" Her voice sank as she said it and it was not like anything he had ever heard before, not in church or Sunday school or when his mother or Miss Erwin told stories. Dorothy Mason sounded as though she had been there. He began to hate intensely Pilate, and the Jews, and Barabbas, but he felt an ashamed hatred for Jesus too, for in a way it seemed to him that Jesus was responsible for all this. And most of all he hated Dorothy Mason. "I wish you'd die, God damn you!" he said silently, through his clenched teeth.

Dorothy Mason's voice was toneless now. "Then Pilate took Our Saviour and scourged Him. That means they beat Him. And the soldiers made a crown of thorns and put it on His head." She raised the circle as high as her arms would reach. Her arms and hands did not look crippled as she held it there, and he saw that it was not barbed wire, but great thorns woven and fastened into a crown.

She said, "These are the kind of thorns they crowned Him with. My father brought them back from the Holy Land and I've made them into a crown." She gazed around the class. He felt her eyes, angry yet forgiving, meet his and pass on, and it seemed not only had she been there, but he had, and Miss Erwin had, everyone in the class, but she forgave them all. And then, with a slow motion, she pulled the crown of thorns down upon her head.

She put her elbow on the table. Her flipper-like hands pointed back at herself. She stared straight ahead with her face calm and white, and she looked as she did when she had a nose bleed and Phyllis was holding a wet towel to the back of her neck and Betty wiping her face. And suddenly he thought that if there was any blood then under the thorns, he would not be able to stand it. He felt he could see it starting, a thin bright red trickle at her temple. But then the buzzer rang for recess, jerking him back from something, and he knew there was no blood.

He rose and edged past Dick Stafford's empty desk. With the others he crowded out of the room into the hall. He went to the drinking fountain, but the water tasted like medicine and he spat it out and moved away to stand alone. Everyone seemed to be standing alone, waiting. Dorothy Mason shuffled out of the room and down the tiled hall toward the fountain. David Kelly, who had been last in line, left it without holding the handle for her.

When the buzzer rang again he returned to his seat. Miss Erwin wasn't in the room yet, and Dorothy Mason had been down the hall at the drinking fountain. The square black box stood closed on her desk. Then on the blackboard he saw that someone had written in sprawling words that covered the entire top of the board: DORTHY MASON IS A ROTTEN STINKING OLD CRIPLE.

He took a deep breath; the room seemed completely still, as though no one were *breathing* now. He stared at the sentence and wondered who had done it. He wished he had. Desperately he wished he had. He told himself that if he'd thought of it he would have written it there himself, and the belief made him feel grown-up and strong and no longer ashamed. He heard the quick rapping of Miss Erwin's heels in the hall, and, almost drowned by it, the familiar, slow dragging sound. His head turned; everyone's head turned. Miss Erwin came in.

He saw her holding the door open for Dorothy Mason. He saw her see the sentence on the blackboard. She let the door slam shut gazing around the class. Her eyes were round and strangely shiny, her mouth was slightly open. In the silence he became aware of the slow pulse of his breath, and as Miss Erwin stood there he felt her harsh, rapid breathing attune itself to his and to the breathing of the class. Then she turned back, as if to open the door, to let Dorothy Mason come in.

But she turned again, as he had known she must. Moving heavily she hurried down the aisle to erase the sentence on the blackboard. He stared at her back, at the chalk stains on the hips of her black skirt, at her arms sweeping the eraser back and forth; he watched the words fade into a long whitish smear, and sighed as he heard the door open and the shuffling steps move down along the aisle.

This story is based on an actual event and an actual person. The unfortunate child who was the original of Dorothy Mason was the victim of a physical disability that was certainly not her fault, but her passive and active aggressions were painful in the extreme to her classmates. She wanted others to feel her pain.

She existed pretty much as I have shown her here. What I remember feeling was hatred and outrage combined with guilt for those emotions focused upon a crippled girl. In the actuality she had nose bleeds, which for some reason the class had to learn to deal with (where was the school nurse?). She brought the thorns from the Holy Land to class, though the crown of them she placed upon her head is fiction. But the thorns were *real* and shocking, the needles about two inches long, stout with a kind of metalling protecting their sharp tips. They made Jesus' crowning with them very real and cruel.

So the "things" I had were some real thorns and the nose bleeds, with the vividness of the blood staining the girl's white skin. The emotions that led to the writing of the story were strong and long lasting.

In the original version of the story the teacher bows to the will of the assembled and holds the door open for Dorothy Mason to come in and view the writing on the blackboard. Miss Erwin was to accede to the class's wish to crucify Dorothy Mason because of the irrevocable damage she had done to comfortable Sunday School feelings about Jesus and Easter.

Editors at *Epoch* magazine, where the story was published, however, did not think that nice, professional Miss Erwin would realistically participate in such an action, so they asked for the change in the ending and I complied.

The point of view here is very close third person. The power of the story, I thought, would be dissipated if there were any more self-awareness than this unnamed boy possesses. The reader is able to see and understand more than the boy does, but the author as explainer stays well away from the action. Nothing violates the sense that the reader is looking at this fifth grade world exactly as the boy does. This (it seems to me) much empowers the dramatic center of the story. When the boy observes Dorothy Mason placing the crown of thorns upon her head, no one tells us what he feels. We know.

The story begins, "He had been awake for some time when he heard his mother calling him." This statement is not the boy's own; the reader will move gradually closer to his consciousness. The second sentence is factual description: "He crossed his arms over his stomach and pressed down hard." The third sentence becomes more closely his in its language: "He was really sick today, all right." The fourth and fifth sentences move even closer: "They wouldn't make him go to school if he was really sick. He wouldn't have to see her sitting there with her nose bleeding now till after Easter vacation, and maybe after Easter his father would get him transferred to Horace Mann Grammar School so that he would never have to see her again at all." These sentences unabashedly set up suspense, and they also bring the reader fully into the boy's consciousness.

The details early in the story establish the boy's orderly world that is being disrupted by the events at school. The father's shoes are shined, underwear is to be found in the top drawer, the pictures to be taken to school are in their proper order. The sterner forms of religiosity are absent in this household, with the Oz books on the shelf, and no doubt an Easter of bunnies and Easter eggs.

The boy's sense of place and unthreatening order are reinforced at school, where Miss Erwin stands before the blackboard, Iris Black and Phyllis Henderson have traded seats; Iris and Betty Andrews sit with Dorothy Mason, to help her with her nose bleeds. Warren Kleinschmidt sits next to the protagonist, Mary Sebastian behind him, Elizabeth Holmes on the other side of Dick Stafford.

Even the regular seating has been disrupted by the requirements of Dorothy Mason, whose coming has changed all that was comfortable into the uncomfortable and guilty. Things will never be the same again.

The structure of the story is that of, say, Sophocles' *Oedipus Rex*. It starts with the now, moves back in time to furnish necessary information, then returns to the present for the resolution. This is simply accomplished by a shift in tense in the ninth paragraph: "She *had* come into the fifth grade a few days after the beginning of the term. He had heard . . . the . . . dragging sound that, although he did not know it then, meant that Dorothy Mason was coming." The next paragraph completes the transition: "Miss Erwin *had* turned quickly . . . picked up her ruler and tapped on her desk with it. She *said*, "There will be . . ."" The story returns from the flashback by the use of the word *now*: "Now as he hurried down the hall . . .""

Certainly the author was conscious of the Christian symbolism. But Dorothy is not Christ as Miss Erwin is not Pontius Pilate (as was suggested in a workshop discussion of the story). Dorothy Mason is a cripple whose defenses take the form of a religious utterance. She refuses to be merely the "little lame girl" of Miss Erwin's euphemism. She seeks to punish others for her own pain, and the religious aspects of the story are most effective when they stem from her distress rather than the author's thematic heavy-handedness.

THE RETAINING WALL

The wall was in the canyon at the end of Hickory street. When I was little I used to think it was there to keep Mission Hills from sliding down into Old Town. The canyon was narrow where the retaining wall was, broadening and dropping away below it to Old Town where poor people lived in little dirty old houses. We weren't supposed to go down to Old Town. All of us— me, John D. and Bobby—had strict orders not to. We weren't supposed to play in the canyon between Mission Hills and Old Town. There were rattlesnakes in the canyon, though none of us had ever seen any, and tramps. We'd all seen tramps. They came up into Mission Hills to ask for a handout, or if they could mow the lawn or wash the car or do any kind of job for a little money. The tramps came up from Old Town.

Our folks wouldn't have let us play at the retaining wall either if they'd known some of the chances we took. It went clear across the canyon, a half a block long and about four feet wide. Even though we played there almost every day that summer I was always scared when I was on that middle part of the retaining wall. The wall was so narrow, and when you looked down it seemed to go forever down, and it bellied a little on the Mission Hills side and swayed in on the other. Rusty hunks of reinforcing steel stuck out of it and you knew if you fell off one of them would go right through you and tear your insides out. And at the bottom there were old tin cans and boards with nails in them and brickbats and junk people from Mission Hills had dumped there, even though a sign said not to, order of the Police Dept. John D. said some day the whole Mission Hills side of the canyon would be filled up to the retaining wall.

For a long time the most daring thing we did was sit on the wall with our legs hanging over and pretend we weren't scared. But I was always scared and I knew Bobby was, and I'll bet John D. was too. Then once we skated across, except we didn't really skate, we just walked across on our skates. It was John D.'s idea so we made him go first. Then I had to go, because he had, and we both yelled chicken at *Bobby* till he did it too. Bobby's face was pretty white when he'd made it over to where we were, and it got white when John D. and I started talking about riding our bikes across. John D. and I said we were going to do it right then, but of course we were just talking big, until that time with Danny.

The first time we saw Danny we were down in the Mission Hills side of the canyon. We'd propped up the old Coca Cola sign and were pegging rocks at it. "Hey, who's that!" Bobby whispered, and I saw this boy sitting on the top of the wall. I knew right away he was from Old Town. He was skinny and was wearing overalls and his bare feet were black on the bottom.

"Hey!" John D. yelled. He sounded surprised. "Hey, you better get down off that retaining wall!"

"I got as much right up here as anybody," the boy said.

"Oh yeah!" John D. said.

"Yeah," the boy from Old Town said. "You want to make me get off!"

"You think I can't!"

"You think you can, fattie?"

John D. looked mad. He wasn't very fat. We all went up on the wall with Bobby lagging behind. Bobby's socks were always falling down into his shoes and he had to stop to pull them back up. The boy from Old Town was littler than John D. or me, not much taller than Bobby, so it wasn't right for John D. to fight him. I told John D. so, but John D. knew that.

"What's your name?" I asked. The boy said his name was Danny. He had buck teeth, and he kept brushing his long hair back whether it needed it or not.

I said my name was Rickey and that was John D., and the other one was Bobby. We all sat down on the wall. "You're from Old Town, aren't you?" John D. said. Danny nodded and let a drool of spit fall down between his legs. It fell a long way before it hit against the wall and made a dark smear.

"That's sure a crummy school down in Old Town," John D. said. "I sure wouldn't go to that school. Everybody in Mission Hills goes to Grant."

"What's the matter with that school down there?" Bobby asked. He was always asking questions like that. John D. scowled at him.

"It's in Old Town, that's what's wrong with it," he said. "Don't you know anything?"

Bobby looked at him, but he shut up. Danny let some more spit fall. I said why didn't we all go back and throw rocks at the Coca Cola sign.

Danny could throw better than any of us and it made John D. mad again. Danny hit the sign nine times out of ten and the best John D. or I could do was eight. Bobby only made five and John D. wouldn't let him throw with the rest of us to see who could hit closest to the top of the wall. This time John D. won.

"I do better than that, mostly," he said. "Once I bounced a big one right off the very top."

"Some guys I know could bounce every one off there left-handed with their eyes shut," *Danny* said. He squinted at John D. "Guys from Old Town."

"Guys from Old Town," John D. said. He curled his fist over his mouth and made a loud *raspberry*. Danny made a louder one and then a long, rolling belch. John D. belched too, but it wasn't as good. Danny put two fingers in his mouth and gave the loudest whistle I'd ever heard. John D. didn't even try to beat it. We couldn't do it at all.

"I know about Old Town guys," he said. "Come up to Mission Hills and want a quarter or a sandwich or something. Mom lets them mow our lawn once in awhile. See if your father wants to come up and mow our lawn. Maybe Mom'll give him a job."

"See if your father wants to come kiss my foot," Danny said. "Maybe I'll give him a job."

"What's your father do?" I asked.

"He works at the olive factory."

"Hey, no kidding?" Bobby said.

I said my father was an insurance agent for the whole San Diego county.

"*My* father's vice president at the bank," John D. said.

"Hey, Danny, what's your father do at the olive factory?" Bobby asked.

"Aaaaah, only old niggers and Mexicans work in the olive factory," John D. said. "I'll bet your father's a tramp."

Danny said something dirty about John D.'s father, and John D. gave him a push so he fell over the Coca Cola sign. Danny jumped up and punched John D. in the stomach, but John D. got him down and was hitting him. We dragged John D. off and held him while Danny got up again. Danny walked off and climbed the side of the canyon. When he turned to spit over his shoulder John D. yelled that he'd better not show up on this side of the retaining wall again, if he knew what was good for him.

But a couple of days later Danny came back and he and John D. got into another fight. John D. won but Danny had given him a bloody nose, and Danny wouldn't take it back about John D.'s father unless John D. took it back about his. So finally John D. said okay, and Danny said okay, too.

We saw Danny a lot after that. Once when John D. had gone to Los Angeles with his folks Danny told Bobby and me he didn't like to play with the Old Town guys. He said the Old Town guys were a pretty bad bunch and if you hung around with them you'd get in trouble with the police, because of the things they'd do. Bobby liked Danny. I liked him all right, but Danny and John D. never got along at all. John D. was always saying things about Old Town and the people who lived there, and then Danny would call John D. fattie, which made John D. mad.

It wasn't fair of Danny to call John D. fattie. The things John D. said about Old Town were all so, and though John D. was fat, he wasn't *very* fat, and if Danny hadn't been from Old Town he'd have known John D. wasn't supposed to beat up on him, because he was smaller than John D. It would be almost as bad as John D. or me hitting Bobby, when Bobby was only eleven.

Once when we were riding our bikes along by the end of Hickory street we saw Danny down at the retaining wall. We yelled at him to come up. "Hey, Danny," I said. "Get your bike and let's go ride around."

"I don't have a bike," Danny said, "—any more." He looked at *my* bike which was new and was better than John D.'s or Bobby's.

"What happened to it?" Bobby asked.

"It got swiped."

"I bet you never had a bike," John D. said.

"I did too," Danny said. "Let's go play down at the retaining wall, you guys."

"You can ride my bike, Danny," Bobby said, but Danny didn't want to. He said his had been swiped a long time ago and he probably couldn't ride any good any more. He said he didn't want to hurt Bobby's bike. I didn't believe he'd ever had a bike either, but I didn't say so.

"If you know how to ride a bike once you always know how," John D. said. He gave his bike a push and swung his leg over the bar. He got going pretty fast and came back steering with his feet on the handlebars. "Hey, can you do this, Rick?" He knew I couldn't. He said to Danny, "Hey, Danny, why don't you get your father to buy you a bike? He could ride around with us sometimes, couldn't he, Rick?"

"I haven't got any use for a bike," Danny said. "That one I had just sat around in the garage all the time. That's why I didn't care when it got swiped."

John D. laughed that way that always made me mad. He started doing smaller and smaller figure eights until he had to catch himself with his foot. "I'll bet none of you guys can do that," he said.

Danny was watching John D. with his head dipped down. His face looked hard around the mouth and his buck front teeth made flat marks on his lower lip. Finally he said, "Let's go down to the wall. I bet I can do something you guys can't do."

We leaned our bikes against the curb and followed him down. He walked out to the middle of the retaining wall without looking back. Then he inched his way over to the edge. He raised his arms in front of him and moved a little more until he was standing on one leg and the other foot was out over the rim of the wall. He did a one-legged deep-knee-bend that way, going down and resting and then coming up slowly with his arms still held out in front of him and his right leg dangling over.

"That's nothing," John D. said. He moved over to the edge and I heard him take a deep breath. He did it too, though he didn't do it as well as Danny had. "That's nothing," John D. panted.

It was my turn now, and I wasn't going to do it. But Danny was looking at John D. with his head dipped down and his mouth hard like that again.

"Bet you can't do this, then," he said. He got down on his hands and knees and backed up until his feet were over the edge, then his knees.

"Hey, don't Danny!" Bobby said. But Danny slid over the side until he was holding just by his hands and elbows. "Hey, you better not," I said. Danny just kept watching John D., sliding down till only his head showed, and his hands that were white like the concrete. He went down until his head was below the top of the retaining wall. I thought he was going to let himself drop, and below him were those rusty reinforcing rods, sticking out like spears, and far down the bottom of the canyon with the broken barrel and the sharp edges of the Coca Cola sign and the brickbats and tin cans.

"Bet you can't do this," Danny grunted. His head moved up again, his face straining and his fingers looking like sticks of chalk trying to dig into the concrete. John D.'s face got strained too, but mad at the same time. When he looked at Bobby and me all of a sudden I thought he was going to jump on Danny's hands and kick them loose, and it scared me worse than what Danny was doing. But then I was ashamed of thinking that about John D.

Danny came up till he could hook his elbows over the edge, and rested there, panting. Bobby whispered, "Hey, we got to help him, you guys."

"You better stay back!" John D. said.

But Bobby had bent down and put out his hand to Danny. He looked up at me. "Hey, Rick." I didn't move. John D. had started around me like he meant to hit Bobby. I didn't know what to do. I thought we'd better help Danny, but I didn't want to get in bad with John D.

"He's got to make it on his own," I said.

"I'll make it," Danny said.

John D. stopped and Bobby backed away. Danny grunted as he swung one leg up and got his heel hooked over the edge of the wall. His foot was white now on the bottom from walking on the concrete wall, but black under the white. Then the foot slipped loose and Bobby yelled. I yelled too. I thought Danny was gone, and I could see those reinforcing rods sticking right through him.

Danny hadn't let go, though. He got his foot up again and moved his heel around till it stuck on something and then his hands scratched in away from the edge. Grunting, the muscles in his neck sticking out and jumping, he boosted himself up till he could roll up and over the edge. He lay there and panted.

When he got to his feet his face was dark and sweaty and the front of him white from rubbing against the concrete. "Bet you can't do that, fattie," he whispered.

I knew John D. wouldn't try it. He didn't look at Danny. But then he said, "I can do something better than that!" He ran back along the wall. We watched him get his bike from the curb and wheel it along the side of the canyon.

He was going to ride his bike across. He was going to start up on the slope above the wall. We'd decided that was the only way to do it, so as to be going fast enough when you hit the wall to steer the bike straight, because otherwise the front wheel would wiggle all around until you got up speed. Bobby and Danny and I moved off the wall while John D. wrestled his bike up the slope. He sat on the seat with his feet planted down and from where we were I could see how red his face was. Danny kept brushing his hand over his hair.

Bobby said, "Oh!" and John D. had started. He came down the slope with his feet stretched out to stop himself, but he hit the retaining wall square and started pedaling. He came fast along it.

The front wheel swung a little at the middle part, so that Bobby said, "Oh!" again, but John D. managed to keep it straight. The bike ran up the slope on our side and John D. tipped over with it when it stopped, and fell down. The front wheel of the bike was still spinning.

John D. got his leg out from under the cross-bar, stood up and brushed off his cords. "Can't do that, can you?" he said to Danny. "Can't do that, can you?" John D. yelled.

"I used to be able to," Danny said. "I could've before somebody swiped my bike."

"You dirty liar!" John D. yelled. "You never had a bike! Your old father couldn't even buy you a bike." He turned on me like he was mad at me too. "Well, come on! You going to try it Rick? You yellow too?"

I said I didn't think I'd try it.

"Chicken! Chicken! Chicken!" John D. yelled. "You better go down to Old Town with buck-teeth Danny. You sure don't belong in Mission Hills, you chicken!"

I just about hit John D., but he'd already licked me twice. I wasn't going to let him say that to me, though. I yelled back, "Okay, then, fattie," and I ran to get on my bike.

Behind me I could hear John D. shouting at Bobby and Danny. He sure thought he was something for riding across that retaining wall. I pushed my bike over to the slope above the wall. I aimed it without looking very close at where I had to go, because I wasn't scared yet. I was still too mad at John D., and I knew I had to do it too. I started down the slope with my feet stuck out before I had time to get scared.

When I hit the wall I pedaled with my head down so out of the corners of my eyes I wouldn't see into the canyon. I didn't even think what I'd do if I started to go off. The top of the wall came at me like a white ribbon winding up under the front wheel of my bike. It seemed to take about three hours to get to the middle, though it seemed too like I was going faster than I'd ever gone on a bike before. But then I was past the middle and I hadn't even let the handlebars wiggle yet. I looked sideways once, to see Old Town so far down there. I could make out the place where they sold tamales on the main street, and the yard of the olive factory where Danny's father worked, where a lot of big, dirty barrels stood in stacks. On my bike, on top of the retaining wall, I was further above Old Town than I had ever been. And now I was scared. It was big and cold in my stomach, and in my legs that were pumping as hard as they could. I was scared of falling, but I was scared because I was going so fast, and because I couldn't stop and I couldn't turn around and go back. But there was John D. at the other end, getting bigger all the time, and like you snap your fingers the feeling about stopping and turning back was gone, and I wasn't scared any more. And I wasn't mad at John D. anymore.

Before I knew it I was going up the slope past him, and past Bobby and Danny. I jumped off when my bike lost speed, so I didn't fall down. I had meant to yell at John D. that I had gone faster than he had, but I didn't feel like that now. I turned toward Danny instead.

Danny was beating it across the retaining wall. I thought he was running home to Old Town and I laughed out loud. But Bobby whispered, "He's going to try it. He's going to use my bike." He sounded like he was crying. John D. stood there with his legs wide apart and his hands in the pockets of his cords. I went up beside him. We watched Danny carry Bobby's bike in front of him along the side of the canyon. He set the bike down on the slope and straddled it.

John D. said calmly, "He won't try it. He doesn't even know how to ride a bike."

I nodded. Bobby didn't say anything. We watched Danny. After a long time I saw the bike start to move. I almost yelled to Danny to stop. Bobby did yell and Danny stopped, turning the bike sharp and falling off it. But he jumped right up on it again as though he just hadn't got started right.

Then John D. began to yell, yelling chicken and yellow, and coward, which was the worst of all, and shouting things about Old Town and Danny's old tramp of a father who couldn't buy him a bike because they were too poor, and couldn't even pay a dentist to get those buck teeth fixed or buy him decent clothes or a haircut like he always needed, and sent him up to Mission Hills to suck around us guys.

Danny was yelling too. He cursed and called John D. names, and he called me and Bobby names too and said things about our fathers. He said dirty things guys in Mission Hills never said, and I wasn't going to take it even if John D. was. I picked up a rock and heaved it toward Danny. It didn't go very far, falling into the canyon, and John D. threw one further.

Danny shut up. He was still sitting on the bike with the front of his shirt and pants dusty white, and he kept running his hand over his hair. I was looking around for another rock when I saw Bobby's face. He was standing a little behind us, staring at John D. and me with his mouth and his eyes wide open. The way he was looking at us made me ashamed. But John D.

threw a couple of more rocks, and I threw another, and I felt better, except that I didn't want to look at Bobby again.

One of John D.'s rocks hit the wall and skipped across. It almost got to Danny. He watched it all the way, and when the rock finally stopped he got off Bobby's bike, picked it up and carried it back to the street. We could still see him as he got on it and started pedaling.We saw him when he fell off, and John D. laughed in that way he had. I laughed too.

John D. said, "He's going to steal that bike."

"I'll bet he is too," I said. I wondered how I could tell John D. I was sorry I'd called him fattie. We walked across the retaining wall with Bobby trailing behind. When we got to the street Danny and Bobby's bike were gone. We went to the corner and looked down the road to Old Town, but we couldn't see them.

"He stole that bike," John D. said.

"We'd better go get our bikes before he steals them, too," I said.

"That thief."

"He'll bring it back," Bobby said.

"That's all you know," John D. said. "You'll never see that bike again."

I said maybe we ought to call the police. John D. said we ought to go to his house and call the police, like it had been his idea in the first place. But I was through being mad at John D.

I stuck close to him as we went up Hickory street to his house.

Bobby kept lagging behind to pull up his socks. He didn't want to come, but we made him. When we told Mrs. Denmuth about the bike at first she wouldn't believe it. But when we told her it was a boy from Old Town who'd been hanging around she got mad and believed us and called the police. The police said they'd be right out. Mrs. Denmuth gave each of us a Milky Way candy bar and we went and sat on the curb to wait. Bobby was crying.

"You'll get your bike back, Bob," I said. "They'll find it."

"They'll catch that dirty thief," John D. said. His jaw worked back and forth as he chewed on the Milky Way. Bobby hadn't unwrapped his yet.

"What do you suppose they'll do to him?" he asked.

I shook my head.

"I know," John D. said.

Bobby and I said, "What?" Bobby was mopping at his nose with the back of his hand.

"They'll put him in the reformatory," John D. said. "And when he gets old enough they'll put him in prison."

Bobby jumped up. He looked from John D. to me; his mouth was hanging open again and he was crying hard. He piled on top of John D., sobbing and yelling, and when I tried to get him off he socked me one on the neck that hurt. But it wasn't really a fight, because I was almost as big as John D. now, and we were a lot stronger than Bobby. It didn't take us long to get him down and sit on him.

Again, the "thing" was real, a retaining wall at the foot of Hickory street in Mission Hills, in San Diego. This had been built in a ravine, to be filled up with dumped dirt and trash in order to make it a buildable lot. It was at least fifty feet high in the center, and very scary looking down from the top, for there were rusty daggers of rebar sticking out from it that would impale you as you fell past. We played around it a lot, scaring ourselves; we never bicycled over it, but we did skate across. It had its fascination, and even then, I think, there was a sense of symbolism.

That edge of Mission Hills, where the prosperous San Diego suburb fell away into Mission Valley and Old Town, was a special place. The time is late Depression. Our fathers were bank managers, hardware store owners, contractors (mine), whose jobs were threatened by the Depression, and so our very existence in that middle-class oasis lay under threat. The Hills formed a kind of rampart (as we thought then) against Old Town below, which was the embodiment of the fall from middle-class grace. Poor people lived and worked in Old Town, Mexican poor people, homeless, unemployed, tramps, bums, unfortunates of the Depression, who sometimes climbed out of their pit to appear on our streets looking for handouts.

"The Retaining Wall" is a social protest story and the characters are political constructs. The young author here let his symbols jump all over him. The retaining wall is a wall holding off Depression Old Town from hanging-on-to-prosperity Mission Hills; it's top is also, from right to left, a passage from youthful innocence to full-fledged no-hostage middle-classism (as I saw it then). The Mission Hills boys are markers on a scale. John D. is a set-in-concrete ruthless, dehumanized bourgeois protecting his endangered superior position in life. Ricky is the boy in motion from childhood innocence and compassion to John D.'s state. Bobby still retains his childish good conscience. The story is didactic in intent.

A major issue in the conception of the story was point of view. In the usual usage of first-person narration there are two time frames, the retrospective time of the taking place of the action and the later or present time when the narrator has come to understand the meanings of that past action in relation to his present situation. There is none of the latter time frame here, and yet (I hoped) it is implicit. Ricky, at some later time, is looking back on the incident where he had to choose what he was to become and *is*. This dramatic incident shows him becoming aware of the unfairness of a situation in which he is participating, along with the discovery that he is committed to the side of the unfairness.

Checklist for Short Stories

1. Is the material appropriate to a short story in its intensity and scope?
2. Does it begin and end where it should?
3. Does the writing appeal to the five senses?
4. Is the action dramatized?
5. Is the focus on particulars?
6. Is the point of view clear and consistent?
7. Is the tension established in the first paragraph?
8. Is there a point of crisis, revelation or recognition?
9. Is the story resolved?
10. Is the characters' speech consistent and revelatory?
11. Is the language of the story appropriate? Abstract or vague? Verbs passive? Modifiers excessive?

Some Notes on the Novella/Novelette/Nouvelle

The novella is commonly described as an extended and complete piece of fiction that is longer than a short story but shorter than a novel. Thus it combines the economy of the short story with the broader scope of the novel.

It is impossible to say where a long short story becomes a novelette, or a novella turns into a short novel. Henry James, who loved the form, defined it as between 18,000 and 45,000 words. He considered it a perfect form for working out a single idea, or following a single emotional arc. I consider a novella's length more flexible than that, like the judge who could not define pornography but knew it when he saw it. A novella is a matter of scope and pace as well as length.

Its length allows a novella more of everything than a short story. Novellas split the difference between short story and novel, with some of the compression of the story and some of the expansion of the novel, although there is no room for novelistic self-indulgence. The novella can sustain deeper explorations of character than a short story but is restricted in plot-lines and settings.

A novella commonly follows a single character through a limited time frame in a limited locale, focusing on a single action, but without the strict economy of a short story. James's nouvelles, Thomas Mann's *Death in Venice*, Kafka's *The Metamorphosis* and Conrad's *The Secret Sharer* can be described this way.

The compactness of the short story is particularly suited to stories of sudden insight and illumination. The novel is better at handling narratives of growth and change. The novella can do both.

Novellas, like short stories, cannot seek to create more than a segment of the world of the novel. The whole picture cannot be shown. Because it moves along a single line of action, the rhythm of narration differs from that of a novel. It is tight and exclusive rather than expansive, and the author must follow a strict standard of relevance when deciding what is to be included.

Since it focuses on a single idea, the author selects a particular story, image or event that will facilitate the exploration of the idea, and must invent, recall or borrow a striking fictional correlative of the idea.

In *A River Runs Through It*, this correlative is fly-fishing. Family, the Code of the West, grace and salvation are all presented in terms of fly-fishing. This novella is not particularly limited in action or in major characters, but the central metaphor does determine what scenes the author has chosen to depict, and the instances in which his characters are portrayed—as about to go fishing, returning from fishing or talking about fishing.

The novella often tends to the archetypal or allegorical. In *Death in Venice*, Aschenbach and Tadzio have archetypal aspects. So does Kurtz in *Heart of Darkness*, Gregor Samsa in *The Metamorphosis*. Often, too, novellas have employed layers of authority. *The Turn of the Screw* and *Heart of Darkness* are both works in which a complexity of the telling process is an important aspect of the whole. James's ghost story is told by someone who heard it from someone else, who is quoting an account written by still another person. *Heart of Darkness* is related by Marlow to someone else, who relates it to us.

Conrad's *The Secret Sharer*, Herman Melville's *Billy Budd*, Tolstoy's *The Death of Ivan Ilych*, James's *The Beast in the Jungle*, *The Aspern Papers* and *Daisy Miller*, Dostoyevsky's *Notes From Underground* and Philip Roth's *Goodbye, Columbus* share themes of loneliness or obsession. The novella can develop such themes better than the short story but not at a length that would overwhelm the reader, as a novel might do.

A novella often serves as the lead story in a collection of short fiction. Publishers may urge the author of such a collection to interconnect the stories by means of a common protagonist and a climactic story so that it becomes a kind of faux novel.

🍃 CHAPTER 10 🍃

The Novel

. . . in which the most thorough knowledge of human nature, the happiest delineation of its varieties, the liveliest effusions of wit and humor are to be conveyed to the world in the best chosen language.

—JANE AUSTEN

John Fowles describes the persistent image that impelled him to begin writing *The French Lieutenant's Woman*:

> A woman stands at the end of a deserted quay and looks out to sea. That was all. The image rose in my mind one morning when I was in bed still half asleep. It responded to no actual incident in my life (or in art) that I can recall. . . .
>
> These mythopoeic "stills" (they seem almost always static) float into my mind very often. I ignore them, since that is the best way of finding whether they really are the door into a new world.
>
> So I ignored this image; but it recurred. Imperceptibly it stopped coming to me. I began deliberately to recall it and try to analyze and hypothesize why it held some sort of immanent power. It was obviously mysterious. It was vaguely romantic. It also seemed, perhaps because of the latter quality, not to belong to today. The woman obstinately refused to stare out of the window of an airport lounge; it had to be this ancient quay. . . . As I happen to live near one, so near that I can see

it from the bottom of my garden, it soon became a specific ancient quay. The woman had no face, no particular degree of sexuality. But she was Victorian; and since I always saw her in the same static long shot, with her back turned, she represented a reproach on the Victorian age, an outcast. I didn't know her crime, but I wished to protect her. That is, I began to fall in love with her. Or with her stance. I didn't know which.

When I was a student at San Diego State College in the first years of World War II, we would see Errol Flynn at dances at the Hotel del Coronado, across the Bay from San Diego. He was a very handsome fellow with a hairline moustache and an arrogant manner about him. He kept his yacht *Sirocco* in San Diego Harbor. There were all kinds of rumors about him—that he was a Nazi agent, a Japanese spy; most persistent were the scandalous rumors of his seductions. One was that he had asked a whole sorority from State College out for a day on the *Sirocco*, and all the girls had had great fun. But two of them had come back later and had "paid the price." No one knew exactly who these girls were, but the rumors continued to gather.

I became fascinated with the idea of the hero of the novel I was considering going out on the *Sirocco* with his girlfriend. This expanded into a larger idea of the virginal girls of my youth being molested, and in fact the idea of molestation as an abstraction—of which young men being molested by the war in which their elders had involved them was the kicker.

This novel in progress, *Homecoming*, I have often quoted in these pages.

A novel published as *The Children of the Sun* came to me in the form of a voice whispering a name in my ear. The name was Cabeza de Vaca, which was slightly familiar, though I didn't really know who he was. I had to look him up in the library. He was a conquistador who had been shipwrecked on the coast of Texas in the sixteenth century and, with two other Spaniards and a Moor servant, made his way across the continent. He wrote a book of his adventures, *Castaways*. The Native Americans called the castaways the children of the sun because they were always heading west into the sun.

I can't imagine what in my unconscious led to that voice in my ear. The only other time I'd heard it was when it whispered to me every morning, "You're killing yourself!" which was advice to quit smoking three packs of cigarettes a day, advice that I also followed.

One year we were living in Cuernavaca, in Mexico. There was a splendid freeway over the mountain to Mexico City, but on a particular occasion we drove the old, winding road. It was the route the Emperor Maxmillian and his Carlotta would take in their royal carriage, halting for a picnic on the way, looking down from the grand heights. On this trip we passed a tight cluster of crosses beside the road. They were made of two-inch pipe, painted blue but red with rust, crowded together in a little plot. With some research I found out what this graveyard was. A foolhardy politician had challenged the handpicked presendential candidate of the brutal dictator Plutarcho Calles. He was having a party for his supporters in a villa in Cuernavaca when the soldiers came for him. They transported him and twelve of his friends in open cars to the site we had happened upon, by night, their hands bound together with barbed wire. They were forced to stand in the illumination of the headlights, chopped down with machine gun fire and buried where they lay.

From that bit of information, and the "facts" of those "things," the thirteen crosses, I went on to write a novel of the Mexican Revolution, *The Adelita*.

What happens after the germ is planted? If all goes well the characters begin to become a part of the writer's life. He dreams of them at night. The characters take on particulars, traits, pasts. Notes are taken and assembled; synopses are attempted. One way of dealing with synopses is writing short ones then expanding them. In other words, write a five-page synopsis, then expand it to ten pages, then to twenty. When he was writing the great novels of his "major phase," *The Wings of the Dove, The Ambassadors* and *The Golden Bowl*, Henry James wrote very long synopses. That of *The Ambassadors* was 20,000 words, and includes all the major scenes. It is interesting, then, that these three *long* novels were published in successive years.

Many writers, however, are wary of synopses because they constrict the imagination.

At some point the actual writing begins. In the famous advice of Raymond Carver, you put down a first sentence, then a second. When stuck, go back and start over. There's a French expression for it, *reculer pour mieux sauter*, "back up for a better jump." Take another run at it. Barriers form. Barriers are swept away! On the other hand don't devote too much care to the opening chapter as often it will be discarded, when it is discovered that the novel can more effectively begin at a later point.

Philip Roth has this to say about beginning a novel:

> Beginning a book is unpleasant. I'm entirely uncertain about the character and the predicament, and a character in his predicament is what I have to begin with. Worse than not knowing your subject is not knowing how to treat it, because that's finally everything. I type out beginnings and they're awful, more of an unconscious parody of my previous book than the breakaway from it that I want. I need something driving down the center of a book, a magnet to draw everything to it—that's what I look for during the first months of writing something new.

As Stephen King puts it in his piece "On Impact," in the June 19 & 26, 2000, issue of *The New Yorker*:

> . . . as my mind reaccustoms itself to the old routine . . . I feel that buzz of happiness, that sense of having found the right words and put them in a line. It's like lifting off in an airplane: you're on the ground, on the ground, on the ground . . . and then you're up, riding on a cushion of air and the prince of all you survey.

The novel had better begin to inhabit the mind of the writer. If one of the characters limps, the author may begin to limp; if one has a stammer, the author may pick it up.

The writing goes on. I keep a page record at first. Three pages on day one, two on day two, eight on day three, a blank on day four, one on day five, up to ten on day X, when I have hit my stride.

Lower your standards and keep going was William Stafford's advice for dominating writer's block.

For many years we lived in a ski resort and knew the manager well. He said there were at least a hundred good reasons for not running the ski lifts each day. He kept them running. There are fifty good reasons for not getting to work on your novel each day. Keep working. Don't take days off. Hemingway's trick was never to quit for the day at the end of a chapter, always to quit in the middle of a passage, when you knew what you would be writing when you came back to it in the morning.

Another handy trick is to make short synopses. What happens in the next few pages, what happens over the next few chapters. This also is an assist to not getting stuck.

The writer of a synopsis is less apt to get stuck than the writer who wings it; however, the point may come where character X has been synopsized to do something that the full-fledged character X, whose character has been developed in some kind of weird collaboration between the author and the character, does not wish to do. It's a legitimate problem.

What about information? In popular fiction information is often of greater importance than the vagaries of the human heart. Consider the information in the following synopsis of the first third of *Princess Daisy* by Judith Krantz:

SYNOPSIS: *Princess Daisy*

In blockbuster popular fiction the characters are rich and beautiful, the settings expensive and exclusive. *Princess Daisy* begins with an attractive young woman arranging for a commercial filming atop the Empire State Building. She is described through an admiring employee's eye. At the end of the scene the author informs the reader that the blonde young woman in her grungy baseball jacket was born Princess Marguerite Alexandrovna Valensky.

The scene shifts to the famous (and real) photographer Phillippe Halsman photographing the beautiful child along with her glamorous parents. Shifts again to the movie star Francesca Vernon being greeted by her fans as she descends the gangplank of the Queen Mary in Cherbourg in 1951, regarded sourly by the (real) Duke and Duchess of Windsor. In Paris she resides at the George V, and departs for Deauville to join the International Set there. We are informed of the exclusivity of Deauville, and introduced to the playboy polo player Prince Valensky. There is considerable insider information on polo and polo players, and Stash Valensky is characterized by his aggressive style of play. There is a dramatic meeting between Daisy's parents-to-be.

Here the story is interrupted to bring us up to date on Francesca. Her father is chairman of the Department of Foreign Languages at Berkeley, but he is from an Italian family of ancient lineage. There is a supply of information on famous Italian families. Francesca's movie career has been marked by affairs with her leading men, never with the real person but with the Prince of Denmark, Romeo, Heathcliff, Marc Antony, Lord Nelson "and a dozen others." In the process she has won an Academy Award.

Prince Stash Valensky and Francesca make love in the stables where the Prince's polo ponies are quartered. Princess Daisy is conceived.

The wedding is held in the Russian Orthodox Cathedral in Paris, with two of Stash's friends holding golden crowns over the heads of the happy pair. The reception is celebrated at the Ritz with the International Set, and Russian and Hollywood aristocracy in attendance; with full information on all these matters.

Now the reader is informed of Stash's parentage and youth. His father, Prince Vasily Alexandrovitch Valensky, was a "man of dauntless presence, high rank and great physical strength (who) had been the veteran of half a hundred affairs with the exquisite ballerinas of the Marinsky Theater. . . ." There is considerable information on Russian aristocracy. Stash's mother, the lovely Princess Titiana, comes down with tuberculosis, and the family moves to Davos. There is information on Rolls-Royces (which are to be of importance to the plot), and on the Russian Revolution, which is taking place offstage. The fourteen year old Stash is introduced to sex by a French Marquise.

Stash begins his career as a polo player and international womanizer. He takes up flying, and there is information on early aviators and airplanes, especially those powered by Rolls-Royce engines. After the death of his parents Stash is to invest his fortune in Rolls-Royce stock.

He joins the RAF, he is a hero in the Battle of Britain, he marries and divorces his first wife, a WAAF.

The novel returns to Switzerland, where Francesca is waiting for her child to be born. These are twins. One of them is Princess Daisy, the other, who is concealed from the mother, is defective from birth.

Discovering that Stash has concealed the fact of the defective child from her and placed it in an institution, Francesca flees to Big Sur. Stash lives morosely in London, occupied with polo and racing planes. We are introduced to Ram, his son by his first, brief marriage. Daisy is enrolled in a British Public (private) School, and the reader is informed of the hierarchies of nobility in such establishments. Francesca dies in an automobile accident in Big Sur, Stash in an airplane crash. After Stash's death the remaining family vacations near Honfleur to consider their Rolls-Royce inheritances. There, about a third of the way through the novel, the seventeen year old Princess Daisy is deflowered by her half-brother.

At this point the synopsist leaves her.

The problems of the very rich are even more complicated and much more glamorous than our own. *Princess Daisy* proceeds compellingly, showing the reader surfaces rather than interiors, but the pace is rapid, the excitement continuous, and the warning bell of crises to come (for instance, the fortune in Rolls-Royce stock) sounds regularly. And the information packed into this novel is truly impressive.

The following passage from James Lee Burke's *Sunset Limited* runs from the beginning to the first space break of chapter one:

> I had seen a dawn like this one only twice in my life: once in Vietnam, after a Bouncing Betty had risen from the earth on a night trail and twisted its tentacles of light around my thighs, and years earlier outside Franklin, Louisiana, when my father and I discovered the body of a labor organizer who had been crucified with sixteen-penny nails, ankle and wrist, against a barn wall.
>
> Just before the sun broke above the Gulf's rim, the wind, which had blown the waves with ropes of foam all night, suddenly died and the sky became as white and brightly grained as polished bone, as though all color had been bled out of the

air, and the gulls that had swooped and glided over my wake lifted into the haze and the swells flattened into an undulating sheet of liquid tin dimpled by the leathery backs of stingrays.

The eastern horizon was strung with rain clouds and the sun should have risen out of the water like a mist-shrouded egg yolk, but it didn't. Its red light mushroomed along the horizon, then rose into the sky in a cross, burning in the center, as though fire were trying to take the shape of a man, and the water turned the heavy dark color of blood. Maybe the strange light at dawn was only coincidence and had nothing to do with the return to New Iberia of Megan Flynn, who, like a sin we had concealed in the confessional, vexed our conscience, or worse, rekindled our envy.

But I knew in my heart it was not coincidence, no more so than the fact that the man crucified against the barn wall was Megan's father and that Megan herself was waiting for me at my dock and bait shop, fifteen miles south of New Iberia, when Clete Purcel, my old Homicide partner from the First District in New Orleans, and I cut the engines on my cabin cruiser and floated through the hyacinths on our wake, the mud billowing in clouds that were as bright as yellow paint under the stern.

It was sprinkling now, and she wore an orange silk shirt and khaki slacks and sandals, her funny straw hat spotted with rain, her hair dark red against the gloom of the day, her face glowing with a smile that was like a thorn in my heart.

Clete stood by the gunnel and looked at her and puckered his mouth. "Wow," he said under his breath.

A common novel beginning is an arrival. In a western a stranger rides into town: The status quo is going to change. A client comes to the private detective's office: An adventure of investigation is about to begin. Here the cabin cruiser is coming into a dock, where an attractive woman from the past with some message or demand or reminder is waiting the arrival of the protagonist.

The passage is packed with information. The protagonist is a boatman, he operates a bait dock in New Iberia, Louisiana. He has served in Vietnam, where he has been wounded by a land mine called a Bouncing Betty. He has also served in the Homicide department of the First District of New Orleans, and his partner there is now his companion on his cabin cruiser. He is a Catholic. As a boy he and his father discovered a labor organizer crucified (with sixteen-penny nails) on the wall of a barn. He has had some kind of relationship with the daughter of the labor organizer, for the sight of her is like a thorn in his heart. We are not told that she is very pretty, but his partner says, "Wow," at the sight of her.

There is a rather extravagant conceit here of this particular dawn, which the protagonist has seen twice before. This has some relation to Napoleon's memorable bloody dawn of Austerlitz, or to the idea of Chinatown in the film of that name. Something bad happened to Jake Gites in Chinatown, and something bad has happened the two previous times the protagonist here has seen this particular dawn. Once he was wounded in Vietnam; once he found the crucified man. Indeed the sunrise attempts to take the form of a crucifixion, and the seawater becomes the color of blood. Something bad is (again) going to happen, and it will involve that back story, for the daughter of that crucified man is waiting at the dock.

Caveat: Flashbacks

Flashbacks as an aid in fiction may have been invented by Ford Madox Ford and Joseph Conrad early in the twentieth century, or may be as old as Homer. A flashback is an effective and efficient device for bringing in scenes from the past that inform present action and character. It is a very pure example of showing rather than telling. Novelists usually galvanize the action with some rousing scenes before switching into the slower pace reminiscence of the flashback.

There are some caveats. Flashbacks tend to become a set piece, too, they often seem a contrivance and they make the reader overly aware of the proscenium arch over the stage of the action. Most of all they tend to bring the main narrative line to a stop.

The writer should be certain he has a very strong line of suspense in operation before he ventures into a flashback.

Here follows a passage from Sands Hall's novel *Catching Heaven*. Maud has escaped a sputtering film career in Hollywood to flee to her sister's town, Marengo, in the Southwest. In an early draft a flashback of an acting class under the direction of the Greek Nikos had depicted the whole film-hopeful scene of Hollywood, the scene so expertly fashioned and slick that the present action stopped dead. In revision the author broke up the flashback as follows. Maud is reading a bulletin board at a Marengo supermarket:

> According to an attractive black and white poster, Fable Mountain Stage Company's production of *Three Sisters* had just closed its month-long run. Maud, impressed with the quality of the poster, wondered what sort of audiences *Three Sisters* had pulled. She would not have thought there would be a market for Chekhov in a town like Marengo. When some students in her acting class had done a scene from *Uncle Vanya*, Nikos had never gotten around to criticising their work, just bawled them out for doing Chekhov at all.
>
> "Why not? Why not? That you have to ask shows why you mangled him, this poor playwright. Why not? Because American actors think his plays are about plot. Plot! Americans are addicted to plot," Nikos shouted. "This is so you don't have to think. You don't have to work, to make connections—why is this character behaving in this way?"
>
> Others besides Maud had their journals and notebooks out, pens skidding across the page. "A story is not about *plot*, a story is about *character*. Character is plot. Chekhov knows this. This is why actors love to work on Chekhov, although most of them, unless they are very smart"—he tapped the side of his head—"don't know that is why. It is all about inner life." *Inner life*, Maud underlined so hard the pen tore the paper: *Character is plot*.
>
> The next production of Fable Mountain Stage Company would be *Charley's Aunt*; they would finish the season with *A Christmas Carol*.

She dawdled through the aisles of the store. The only interesting cheese she could find was a mild Cheddar. There was
no "interesting" bread, as her mother called it. What French
bread there was was pre-sliced. "A good play it is like holding
a great hunk of rye in your hand," Nikos said. . . .

The miniflashbacks are keyed into the narrative by means of the Chekhov poster and then the "interesting" bread in alternation with the present
scene. This method seems much more believable than a full-scale scene
from the past would be.

The Process

I am presently contemplating a mystery novel set in 1890s San Francisco,
and I have these research items to work from. I am interested in the Chinese
slave girls. These were prostitutes, very young, brought from a China that
looked on female babies as a drag on the family economy; they were at
least lucky not to have been disposed of at birth. Five and ten years after
Lincoln's Emancipation Proclamation these ten- to twelve-year-old sex
slaves were still being imported to San Francisco's Chinatown, the arrival
of a boatload treated in the newspapers like any other commodity from
China, such as rice or camphorwood chests. The prettiest girls were sold
off to wealthy merchants as concubines; the less attractive went into the
terrible cribs of Chinatown.

It is particularly ironic that present-day college admissions officers are
amazed at the elegant GPAs and towering SATs of Chinese girl high
schoolers.

At any rate there was in the 1890s a Scottish woman in San Francisco,
Donaldina Cameron, who devoted her life to liberating these girls from
their captivity, by hook and crook, law or larceny, and up-the-close-and-
down-the-stair hugger-mugger rescues.

Young William Randolph Hearst, son of the fabulously wealthy George
Hearst and the prim Phoebe Apperson Hearst, was a boisterous Harvard
student. When a fellow Californian had to leave the university for financial
reasons, abandoning his mistress, Tessie Powers, Willie Hearst stepped in

and took over the girl, who, although she had been a barmaid, was of some gentility. When he was kicked out of Harvard for his pranks, Willie was employed for a time by Joseph Pulitzer on his *New York World,* then returned to San Francisco where he talked his father into giving him control of the *Examiner,* a failing newspaper the older Hearst had acquired to aid his political career. Willie promptly went into action along the lines he had learned from Pulitzer to make the *Examiner* a great newspaper. He hired the best talent available, including Ambrose Bierce, and devised publicity tricks to jump the circulation.

Willie had brought Tessie with him and installed her in a house, Sea Point, in Sausalito across the Bay. He commuted to San Francisco in his steam yacht.

Sausalito at that time had an international and playboy reputation. There was a large British colony, also a considerable Azorean Portuguese population. Wealthy San Franciscans kept their yachts at the San Francisco Yacht Club anchorage in Sausalito, and the five o'clock ferry from the City was always crowded with pretty young women coming across to parties on the yachts.

Willie and Tessie were not a part of the social scene, and Tessie was referred to as "dirty drawers." At this time Willie was interested in photography, and the second floor at Sea Point was devoted to darkroom and photographic studio, with a resident photographer.

Willie's mother was deeply distressed by the presence of Tessie in her son's life and tried to get rid of her. She eventually succeeded, after an interview with Tessie in a San Francisco Hotel, at what was rumored to be a cost of $150,000. Willie's heart was broken for a considerable period by Tessie's departure.

Why was Tessie Powers called dirty drawers? Was it disapproval of her unmarried situation, or because the term rhymes with her name? The photographer upstairs was not Eadweard Muybridge, but he could be fictionally interested in the same kind of experimentation as Muybridge. It was Muybridge who in a way invented the motion picture when he was hired by Leland Stanford to discover if all a horse's hooves were off the ground at the same time at a gallop. (The answer is yes.) With his system of electrically actuated gangs of cameras, he then went on to photograph other animals in motion, and then naked men, and later women—walking, running, carrying pails, mounting ladders—for large volumes of collected photographs. In a journal entry he writes an apology that the young women he could hire for these photographs were not "cultivated" and thus were perhaps less graceful than cultivated females would be. (They were Philadelphia prostitutes.)

So nude pornographic photographs? A stack of these can be made to resemble a motion picture when flipped rapidly. Willie was interested in many things, mainly collecting (mummies at this time). Might this collecting fever be extended? To what? Or perhaps the house photographer has interests of his own?

How to connect the Sausalito activities with those in Chinatown of my fictional Donaldina and her lover, my protagonist? High jinks and murders among the yachting set? A Donaldina sister in the fast society in Sausalito? A connection of Donaldina with Tessie? A connection through photography: Muybridge and a fictional Arnold Gente, the photographer of early day Chinatown?

Ambrose Bierce employed by Willie's mother to get rid of Tessie? Or to cover up a situation she has provoked by trying to get rid of Tessie? To solve a murder or murders? Of whom?

Item: What of Tessie's previous lover at Harvard?

Item: There were abandoned mines in the hills behind Sausalito.

Item: The Portuguese have a grand colorful celebration of the Holy Ghost each year in Sausalito, with a queen.

Only connect.

A Note on Endings

It is of course much easier to tie up all the loose ends in a short story or short novel, not so easy in a long one, nor is it necessary to deal neatly with all the plotlines so long as the major ones are covered. Endings of huge novels, such as *War and Peace* or James Michener's *Hawaii,* are almost always inadequate because there has been just too much material presented to wrap up without the ending seeming inadequate to the whole.

The following scene is from Louisa May Alcott's *Little Women*. Jo has written a novel:

> Having copied her novel for the fourth time, read it to all her confidential friends, and submitted it with fear and trembling to three publishers, she at last disposed of it, on condition that she would cut it down one-third, and omit all the parts she particularly admired.
>
> ". . . Fame is a very good thing to have in the house, but cash is more convenient; so I wish to take the sense of the meeting on this important subject," said Jo, calling a family council.
>
> "Don't spoil your book, my girl, for there is more in it than you know, and the idea is well worked out. Let it wait and ripen," was her father's advice; and he practiced as he preached, having waited patiently thirty years for fruit of his own to ripen, and being in no haste to gather it, even now, when it was sweet and mellow.
>
> "It seems to me that Jo will profit more by making the trial than by waiting," said Mrs. March. "Criticism is the best test of such work, for it will show her both unsuspected merits and faults, and help her to do better next time. We are too partial, but the praise and blame of outsiders will prove useful, even if she gets but little money."
>
> "Yes," said Jo, knitting her brows, "that's just it; I've been fussing over the thing so long. I really don't know whether it is good, bad, or indifferent. It will be a great help to have cool, impartial persons take a look at it, and tell me what they think of it."
>
> "I wouldn't leave out a word of it; you'll spoil it if you do, for the interest of the story is more in the minds than in the actions of the people, and it will be all a muddle if you don't explain as you go on," said Meg, who firmly believed that the book was the most remarkable novel ever written.
>
> "But Mr. Allen says, 'Leave out the explanations, make it

brief and dramatic, and let the characters tell the story,' " interrupted Jo, turning to the publisher's note.

"Do as he tells you; he knows what will sell, and we don't. Make a good, popular book, and get as much money as you can. By and by, when you've got a name, you can afford to digress, and have philosophical and metaphysical people in your novels," said Amy, who took a strictly practical view of the subject.

"Well," said Jo, laughing, "if my people *are* 'philosophical and metaphysical' it isn't my fault, for I know nothing about such things, except what I hear father say, sometimes. If I've got some of his wise ideas jumbled up with my romance, so much the better for me. Now, Beth, what do you say?"

"I should like to see it printed *soon*," was all Beth said, and smiled in saying it; but there was an unconscious emphasis on the last word, and a wistful look in the eyes that never lost their childish candor, which chilled Jo's heart, for a minute, with a foreshadowing fear, and decided her to make her little venture "soon."

So, with Spartan firmness, the young authoress laid her first-born on her table, and chopped it up as ruthlessly as any ogre. In the hope of pleasing every one, she took every one's advice; and, like the old man and his donkey in the fable, suited nobody.

Her father liked the metaphysical streak which had unconsciously got into it, so that was allowed to remain, though she had her doubts about it. Her mother thought that there *was* a trifle too much description, therefore, it nearly all came out, and with it many necessary links in the story. Meg admired the tragedy, so Jo piled up the agony to suit her, while Amy objected to the fun, and, with the best intentions in life, Jo quenched the sprightly scenes which relieved the sombre character of the story. Then, to complete the ruin, she cut it down one-third, and confidingly sent the poor little romance, like a picked robin, out into the big, busy world, to try its fate.

This scene is delightful because every March makes a comment on Jo's manuscript that is totally in keeping with his or her character. The manuscript suffers accordingly, becoming a "picked robin." In these times manuscripts of short stories or novels do not become "picked robins" in the bosom of the family, but more often in college workshops or summer writers conferences amongst the writer's peers, some of whom wish that MSS well, and some of whom do not.

Let us have a last look at the robin before it flies off.

1. Can the term "luminous particularity" be applied to the prose? That is, is it so specific that the dark corridors of text and character are illuminated?
2. Is it sensuous? That is: are the readers senses engaged?
3. Are the verbs and nouns strong, adjectives only the choicest, rarely used adverbs burnished to glow like jewels?
4. Are the indirections and symbols powerfully suggestive and implicatory?
5. Is the dialogue crisp, brief, and loaded with between-the-lines implications essential to character development and plotline?
6. Has the point-of-view problem been solved as simply and effectively as possible, so that the reader is powerfully coaxed by a voice within the story to follow the destinies of the characters?
7. Are the characters strong, original and perhaps obsessive? Are they *interesting*? Do they initiate the action rather than being acted upon?
8. Does the plot spring from the desires and obsessions, and the actions, of those characters?

Bon voyage!

⚞ Appendix: Suggested Reading ⚟

Fiction Lists

Here is a very personal list of fiction that should be read by writers serious about their craft:

Jane Austen, *Pride and Prejudice, Sense and Sensibility*

Saul Bellow, *The Adventures of Augie March, Henderson the Rain King*

Jorge Luis Borges, *Labyrinths*

Albert Camus, *The Stranger*

Joyce Cary, *The Horse's Mouth*

Willa Cather, *My Antonia*

Miguel de Cervantes, *Don Quixote*

John Cheever, Stories

Anton Chekhov, Stories

Joseph Conrad, *Heart of Darkness*

Charles Dickens, *Great Expectations, Bleak House*

Fyodor Dostoyevsky, *The Brothers Karamazov, The Idiot*

George Eliot, *Middlemarch*

Ralph Ellison, *Invisible Man*

William Faulkner, *The Sound and the Fury, As I Lay Dying, Absalom, Absalom, Light in August,* "The Bear"

F. Scott Fitzgerald, *The Great Gatsby*

Gustave Flaubert, *Madame Bovary*

E.M. Forster, *Howard's End*

Ernest Hemingway, *In Our Time, The Sun Also Rises, A Farewell to Arms,* Stories

Franz Kafka, Stories

Henry James, *The Portrait of a Lady, The Ambassadors*

James Joyce, *Dubliners, A Portrait of the Artist as a Young Man*
D.H. Lawrence, Stories, Novelettes
Norman Mailer, *The Naked and the Dead, The Executioner's Song*
Thomas Mann, *The Magic Mountain*, Stories
Gabriel García Márquez, *One Hundred Years of Solitude*
Herman Melville, *Moby Dick, Billy Budd*
Vladimir Nabokov, *Pale Fire, Lolita*
Flannery O'Connor, Stories
John O'Hara, *Appointment in Samarra*, Stories
Marcel Proust, *Swann's Way*
Thomas Pynchon, *Gravity's Rainbow*
Alain Robbe-Grillet, *The Voyeur*
Juan Rulfo, *Pedro Paramo*
Sir Walter Scott, *Ivanhoe*
Stendhal, *The Red and the Black*
Laurence Sterne, *Tristram Shandy*
Leo Tolstoy, *War and Peace, Anna Karenina*
Ivan Turgenev, *Fathers and Sons*
Mark Twain, *The Adventures of Huckleberry Finn*
Robert Penn Warren, *All the King's Men*

Here is a list of the one hundred best English-language novels of the twentieth century, as drawn up by the editorial board of the Modern Library:

1. *Ulysses*, James Joyce
2. *The Great Gatsby*, F. Scott Fitzgerald
3. *A Portrait of the Artist as a Young Man*, James Joyce
4. *Lolita*, Vladimir Nabokov
5. *Brave New World*, Aldous Huxley
6. *The Sound and the Fury*, William Faulkner
7. *Catch-22*, Joseph Heller
8. *Darkness at Noon*, Arthur Koestler
9. *Sons and Lovers*, D.H. Lawrence
10. *The Grapes of Wrath*, John Steinbeck
11. *Under the Volcano*, Malcolm Lowry
12. *The Way of All Flesh*, Samuel Butler

13. *1984*, George Orwell

14. *I, Claudius*, Robert Graves

15. *To the Lighthouse*, Virginia Woolf

16. *An American Tragedy*, Theodore Dreiser

17. *The Heart Is a Lonely Hunter*, Carson McCullers

18. *Slaughterhouse-Five*, Kurt Vonnegut

19. *Invisible Man*, Ralph Ellison

20. *Native Son*, Richard Wright

21. *Henderson the Rain King*, Saul Bellow

22. *Appointment in Samarra*, John O'Hara

23. *U.S.A.* (trilogy), John Dos Passos

24. *Winesburg, Ohio*, Sherwood Anderson

25. *A Passage to India*, E.M. Forster

26. *The Wings of the Dove*, Henry James

27. *The Ambassadors*, Henry James

28. *Tender Is the Night*, F. Scott Fitzgerald

29. *Studs Lonigan* (Trilogy), James T. Farrell

30. *The Good Soldier*, Ford Madox Ford

31. *Animal Farm*, George Orwell

32. *The Golden Bowl*, Henry James

33. *Sister Carrie*, Theodore Dreiser

34. *A Handful of Dust*, Evelyn Waugh

35. *As I Lay Dying*, William Faulkner

36. *All the King's Men*, Robert Penn Warren

37. *The Bridge of San Luis Rey*, Thornton Wilder

38. *Howard's End*, E.M. Forster

39. *Go Tell It on the Mountain*, James Baldwin

40. *The Heart of the Matter*, Graham Greene

41. *Lord of the Flies*, William Golding

42. *Deliverance*, James Dickey

43. *A Dance to the Music of Time*, Anthony Powell

44. *Point Counterpoint*, Aldous Huxley

45. *The Sun Also Rises*, Ernest Hemingway

46. *The Secret Agent*, Joseph Conrad

47. *Nostromo*, Joseph Conrad

48. *The Rainbow*, D.H. Lawrence

49. *Women in Love*, D.H. Lawrence

50. *Tropic of Cancer,* Henry Miller

51. *The Naked and the Dead*, Norman Mailer

52. *Portnoy's Complaint*, Philip Roth

53. *Pale Fire*, Vladimir Nabokov

54. *Light in August*, William Faulkner

55. *On the Road*, Jack Kerouac

56. *The Maltese Falcon*, Dashiell Hammett

57. *Parade's End*, Ford Madox Ford

58. *The Age of Innocence*, Edith Wharton

59. *Zuleika Dobson*, Max Beerbohm

60. *The Moviegoer*, Walker Percy

61. *Death Comes to the Archbishop*, Willa Cather

62. *From Here to Eternity*, James Jones

63. *The Wapshot Chronicle*, John Cheever

64. *The Catcher in the Rye*, J.D. Salinger

65. *A Clockwork Orange*, Anthony Burgess

66. *Of Human Bondage*, W. Somerset Maugham

67. *Heart of Darkness*, Joseph Conrad

68. *Main Street*, Sinclair Lewis

69. *The House of Mirth*, Edith Wharton

70. *The Alexandria Quartet*, Lawrence Durrell

71. *A High Wind in Jamaica*, Richard Hughes

72. *A House for Mr. Biswas*, V.S. Naipaul

73. *The Day of the Locust*, Nathanael West

74. *A Farewell to Arms*, Ernest Hemingway

75. *Scoop*, Evelyn Waugh

76. *The Prime of Miss Jean Brodie*, Muriel Spark

77. *Finnegan's Wake*, James Joyce

78. *Kim*, Rudyard Kipling

79. *A Room With a View*, E.M. Forster

80. *Brideshead Revisited*, Evelyn Waugh

81. *The Adventures of Augie March*, Saul Bellow

82. *Angle of Repose*, Wallace Stegner

83. *A Bend in the River*, V.S. Naipaul

84. *The Death of the Heart*, Elizabeth Bowen

85. *Lord Jim*, Joseph Conrad

86. *Ragtime*, E.L. Doctorow

87. *The Old Wives' Tale*, Arnold Bennett

88. *The Call of the Wild*, Jack London

89. *Loving*, Henry Green

90. *Midnight's Children*, Salman Rushdie

91. *Tobacco Road*, Erskine Caldwell

92. *Ironweed*, William Kennedy

93. *The Magus*, John Fowles

94. *Wide Sargasso Sea*, Jean Rhys

95. *Under the Net*, Iris Murdoch

96. *Sophie's Choice*, William Styron

97. *The Sheltering Sky*, Paul Bowles

98. *The Postman Always Rings Twice*, James M. Cain

99. *The Ginger Man*, J.P. Donleavy

100. *The Magnificent Ambersons*, Booth Tarkington

There were numerous complaints about this Modern Library list when it was publicized, one of them the fact that it parallels rather closely the Modern Library Publications List.

The following lists are from David Wallechinsky's *The Book of Lists*.

Somerset Maugham's list of the ten greatest novels:

1. *War and Peace* by Leo Tolstoy

2. *Pere Goriot* by Honore de Balzac

3. *Tom Jones* by Henry Fielding

4. *Pride and Prejudice* by Jane Austen

5. *The Red and the Black* by Stendhal

6. *Wuthering Heights* by Emily Brontë

7. *Madame Bovary* by Gustave Flaubert

8. *David Copperfield* by Charles Dickens

9. *The Brothers Karamazov* by Fyodor Dostoyevsky

10. *Moby Dick* by Herman Melville

These are all nineteenth-century novels, and only two by Americans, but of course Maugham was very much British and Victorian.

Here's a list by an American, Clifton Fadiman:

1. *Tom Jones* by Henry Fielding
2. *Ulysses* by James Joyce
3. *The Magic Mountain* by Thomas Mann
4. *Gargantua and Pantagruel* by François Rabelais
5. *Remembrance of Things Past* by Marcel Proust
6. *Moby Dick* by Herman Melville
7. *The Adventures of Huckleberry Finn* by Mark Twain
8. *Don Quixote* by Miguel de Cervantes
9. *The Brothers Karamazov* by Fyodor Dostoyevsky
10. *War and Peace* by Leo Tolstoy

Malcolm Cowley (also American) lists the greatest novelists:

1. Leo Tolstoy
2. Fyodor Dostoyevsky
3. Charles Dickens
4. Miguel de Cervantes
5. Marcel Proust
6. Herman Melville
7. Stendhal
8. Thomas Mann
9. James Joyce
10. Lady Murasaki

Anna Quindlen, in *How Reading Changed My Life*, lists her favorite novels in several categories.

"Books I Would Save in a Fire (If I Could Save Only 10)" eight are novels:

Pride and Prejudice by Jane Austen
Bleak House by Charles Dickens
Anna Karenina by Leo Tolstoy
The Sound and the Fury by William Faulkner
The Golden Notebook by Doris Lessing

Middlemarch by George Eliot
Sons and Lovers by D.H. Lawrence
The House of Mirth by Edith Wharton

"Books I Just Love to Read and Always Will" (nine are novels):
Main Street by Sinclair Lewis
My Antonia by Willa Cather
The Lion, the Witch, and the Wardrobe by C.S. Lewis
Wuthering Heights by Emily Brontë
Jane Eyre by Charlotte Brontë
The Group by Mary McCarthy
The Phantom Tollbooth by Norman Juster
A Christmas Carol by Charles Dickens
Scoop by Evelyn Waugh

"10 Big Thick Wonderful Books That Could Take You a Whole Summer to Read (but Aren't Beach Books)" (nine are novels):
Gone With the Wind by Margaret Mitchell
Vanity Fair by William Makepeace Thackeray
East of Eden by John Steinbeck
The Forsyte Saga by John Galsworthy
Buddenbrooks by Thomas Mann
Can You Forgive Her? by Anthony Trollope
Sophie's Choice by William Styron
Henry and Clara by Thomas Mallon
Lonesome Dove by Larry McMurtry

Valuable Nonfiction Texts

Aristotle, *Poetics*
Erich Auerbach, *Mimesis*
Wayne Booth, *The Rhetoric of Fiction*
Raymond Carver, *Fires*
Carol Edgarian and Tom Jenks, *The Writers Life*
E.M. Forster, *Aspects of the Novel*

Sigmund Freud, *Civilization and Its Discontents*
John Gardner, *On Moral Fiction* and *On Becoming a Novelist*
William Gass, *Fiction and the Figures of Life*
Oakley Hall, *The Art and Craft of Novel Writing*
Henry James, *The Art of the Novel*
Anne Lamott, *Bird By Bird*
Flannery O'Connor, *Mystery and Manners*
Frank O'Connor, *The Lonely Voice*
George Plimpton, ed., *Writers at Work, The Paris Review Interviews*
Theodore Solotaroff, *A Few Good Voices in My Head*
Eudora Welty, *One Writer's Beginnings*

It is clear that different writers are turned on by different novels. I think the above selections of Dickens are crazy. *Great Expectations* is to my mind his best novel. Faulkner's "The Bear" may be a novelette rather than a novel, but I would choose it any day over *The Sound and the Fury,* and *As I Lay Dying*, as well. I'm glad someone finally mentioned *Jane Eyre*, from which whole genres of fiction have evolved, but where is Henry James's *The Portait of a Lady*, many a writer's (mine, too) favorite novel? If I could raise the stock of *Portrait* by grinding up *Wuthering Heights* and scattering the atoms over the world's libraries, I would set out for Haworth with a novel grinder.

Should writers have read all these novels? Yes, they should have. But there will probably be different kinds of novels entirely that will ignite individual fires. The novels that turned me into a novelist were Raymond Chandler's *Farewell, My Lovely* and *The Big Sleep*, and Dashiell Hammett's *The Maltese Falcon*, followed by Hemingway's stories and early novels, followed by Faulkner and Henry James. I'd read some Dickens, of course, and *Vanity Fair* at an early age, but I didn't discover the great Victorians and the Russians until much later, when I decided that I simply had to read everything I should have read.

☙ Index ☙

Stegner, Wallace, 212
Stein, Gertrude, 42
Steinbeck, John, 43, 210, 215
Stendhal, 151, 210, 213, 214
Stephenson, Neal, 13
Sterne, Laurence, 210
Stone, Robert, 104-105, 153
Stranger, The (Camus), 209
Studs Lonigan (Farrell), 211
Styron, William, 25, 213, 215
Sun Also Rises, The (Hemingway), 151, 156, 209, 211
Sunset Limited (Burke), 199-200
Suspension of disbelief, 83
Swann's Way (Proust), 20, 210
Symbols, 47-51, 179, 189
Synopsis, 195, 197

Tale of Two Cities, A (Dickens), 42
Tale of the Unknown Island, The (Saramago), 72
Tarkington, Booth, 213
Templeton, Edith, 165
Tender Is the Night (Fitzgerald), 211
Test plot, 143
Thackeray, William Makepeace, 7, 49-50, 215
"Then Road to Balbriggan" (Newman), 70
Third-person point of view, 95-101
This Side of Paradise (Fitzgerald), 89
Thoughts, interiorization and, 128-129
Three-act structure, 156
Ticking Clock, 157-158
Tidewater Morning, A (Styron), 25-26
Time Crunch, 157-158
To Kill a Mockingbird (Lee, H.), 154
To the Lighthouse (Woolfe), 211
Tobacco Road (Caldwell), 213
Tolkein, J.R.R., 145
Tolstoy, Leo, 131, 147, 192, 210, 213, 214
Tom Jones (Fielding), 213

Toole, John Kennedy, 69
Tosca (Puccini), 149
Tragedy of Hamlet, Prince of Denmark (Shakespeare), 57
Treasure Island (Hawkins), 40-41, 88-89, 95
Tristam Shandy (Sterne), 210
Trollope, Anthony, 215
Tropic of Cancer (Miller), 212
True Grit (Portis), 93, 94
Turgenev, Ivan, 210
Turn of the Screw, The (James, H.), 192
Twain, Mark, 84, 210, 214
Tyler, Anne, 129, 131

U.S.A. (Doss Passos), 211
Ulysses (Joyce), 145, 210
Under the Net (Murdoch), 213
Under the Volcano (Lowry), 210
Underworld (DeLillo), 83, 154
Unofficial Rose, An (Murdoch), 147
Upstairs, Downstairs, 153

Vaca, Cabeza de, 194
Valley of Decision, The (Davenport), 30
Vanity Fair (Thackeray), 7, 49-50, 147, 215, 216
Verbs, 31-32
Volcano Lover, The (Sontag), 21
Voltaire, 27
Vonnegut, Kurt, 211
Voyeur, The (Robbe-Grillet), 210

Walker, Alice, 12, 94
Wallenchinsky, David, 213
Wapshot Chronicle, The (Cheever), 212
War and Peace (Tolstoy), 2-5, 131, 147, 210, 213
Warlock (Hall), 83, 149
Warren, Robert Penn, 210, 211
Waterworks, The (Doctorow), 10
Waugh, Evelyn, 151, 211, 212, 215
Way of all Flesh, The (Butler), 210